Finding
the
Big Thicket:
A Cartographic Approach

Pete A. Y. Gunter

ISBN: 978-1-51682-749-7

Photos by Roy Hamric, taken from *The Big Thicket: A Challenge for Conservation*, Pete A. Y. Gunter

Maps: Stephen Ramsey, Editing by Keith W. Brown

Book design: Dean Fetzer, www.gunboss.com

Contents

Introduction

Just where is the Big Thicket? For some the densely wooded Southeast Texas region is a creation of mere folklore: of vague reminiscence, of tall tales, of typical Texas exaggeration. For others, it is a projection of covetous environmentalists who want to build a fence around it and keep people out: especially lumber company people. For still others, it is an important biological resource, a fabric of varied, interwoven plant growth communities sustaining a rich variety of life. Each of these viewpoints and others that could be mentioned provide mutually inconsistent answers to the question of the Big Thicket's location and character. Clearly, a convincing answer to this longstanding question has not been easy to give.

The present essay is, nonetheless, an attempt to give such an answer. The method used systematically will be cartographic and comparative. This is the first time this method has been used in relation to the Big Thicket. To locate the "Thicket" and describe its character will involve making comparisons of all the proposed maps of that region which the author, after many years of searching, has been able to find. In comparing different locale descriptions, use will be made of "composite" maps: combinations of two or more maps into one. No attempt will be made to present maps in terms of chronological order or size, or assumptions used in making them. The goal is to show, by using these maps in their totality, that, large or small, they converge to a common area: a single Big Thicket region stretching west from the Louisiana border to the southwestern limits of the Southern pine belt.

A final piece will be added to the cartographic puzzle. This will involve consideration of a floristic map by Professor Claude A. McLeod—different from previous maps based on history, folklore, broad regional preconceptions or personal memory. The result of meticulous, detailed observation and a profound understanding of plant ecology, McLeod's map of the Big Thicket's character and borders constitutes a striking advance over all previous descriptions. Its comparison with previous large-scale maps of the region reveals a single (and now biologically intelligible) fundamental insight into the Big Thicket's size, location and nature.

Several consequences follow from this approach. The first involves the relations between science and folklore. While these are often thought to be antithetical and have sometimes proved to be antithetical in political debates, the result of this essay will be to find a rapprochement between them. The second consequence, prospective instead of retrospective, involves the locale of the Big Thicket National Biological Preserve. Created in 1974, this first biological preserve in the history of the National Park System is located almost entirely in the Lower Neches River Drainage Basin. When a map of the preserve is superimposed on McLeod's map it becomes clear that the preserve is located in the center of the original Big Thicket, leaving out its eastern and western regions. This is important, since large areas of the eastern and western Big Thicket remain as possibilities for conservation. Another possibility is made clear by this map: the extension of the preserve's system of stream courses and nature preserves north to create a Neches National Wild and Scenic River. This essay will end with a brief survey of these possibilities.

1. Initial Large Scale Maps

The first two maps are the largest. Price Daniel's expansive gesture covers over nineteen counties and parts of thirteen others: an area more than twice the size of the state of Maryland.[1] The reasons for this excess are political. Daniel's used his map in his fourth and unsuccessful run for governor of Texas in 1962.

It is presented here as a "limit case": the largest boundaries ever proposed for the Big Thicket.

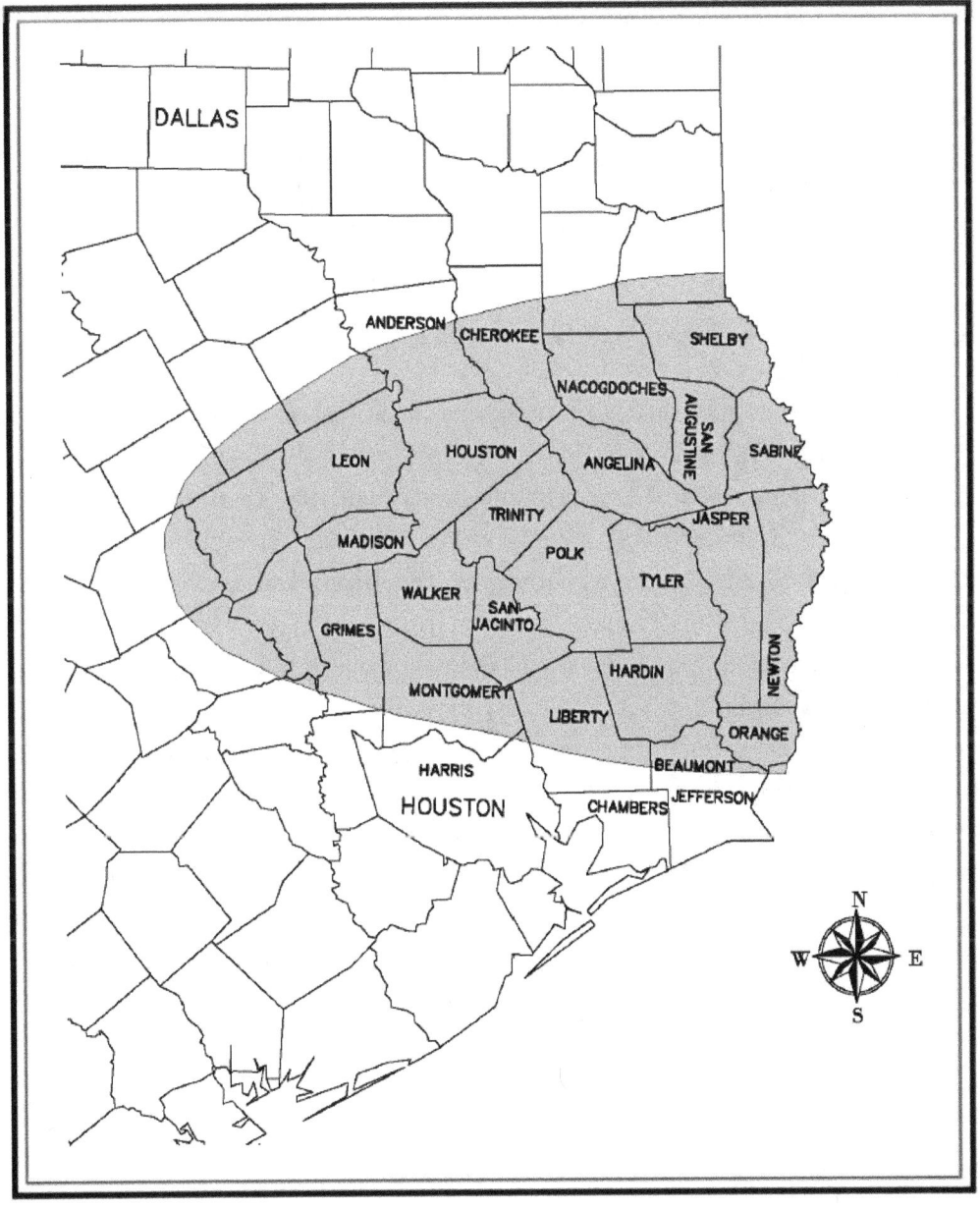

FIG. 1: GOVERNOR PRICE DANIELS
PROPOSED STATE PARK AREA

5

The Big Thicket Biological Survey produced the second map. Done by faculty at Sam Houston State Teachers College (now Sam Houston State University) in 1936, its aim was to provide a scientific justification for the creation of a Big Thicket National Park.[2] More modest than Daniel's later vision, it nonetheless described an original Big Thicket of 3,500,000 acres, approximately 1,000,000 acres of which were declared still to be primitive, largely untouched, wilderness. The biological survey map is given below (as a composite) along with Price Daniel's (Figure 2).

The 1936 survey gave conservationists a botanical and zoological basis which they badly needed to justify a Big Thicket National Park. Boundaries were spelled out along with geographical and edaphic (soil) histories. Lists of plants, reptiles, mammals, birds, fish, spiders, insects were provided, stretching in small type across 36 pages. Useful as it was, however, the Biological Survey had problems. The borders of the Big Thicket were mapped, but no explanation of these borders was provided, beyond saying that they were Pliocene in their origins. Lists of flora and fauna were sometimes gathered from research in the Big Thicket, but more often were read of from textbook descriptions of species distributions. Carelessness did sometimes intervene. The author discovered a reference in the 1936 survey to the existence of wavyleaf oak in the Thicket. But to find an actual specimen of that oak, one would need to range as far afield as far West Texas or Nevada. If the Survey was at least a first start, it left much to conjecture.

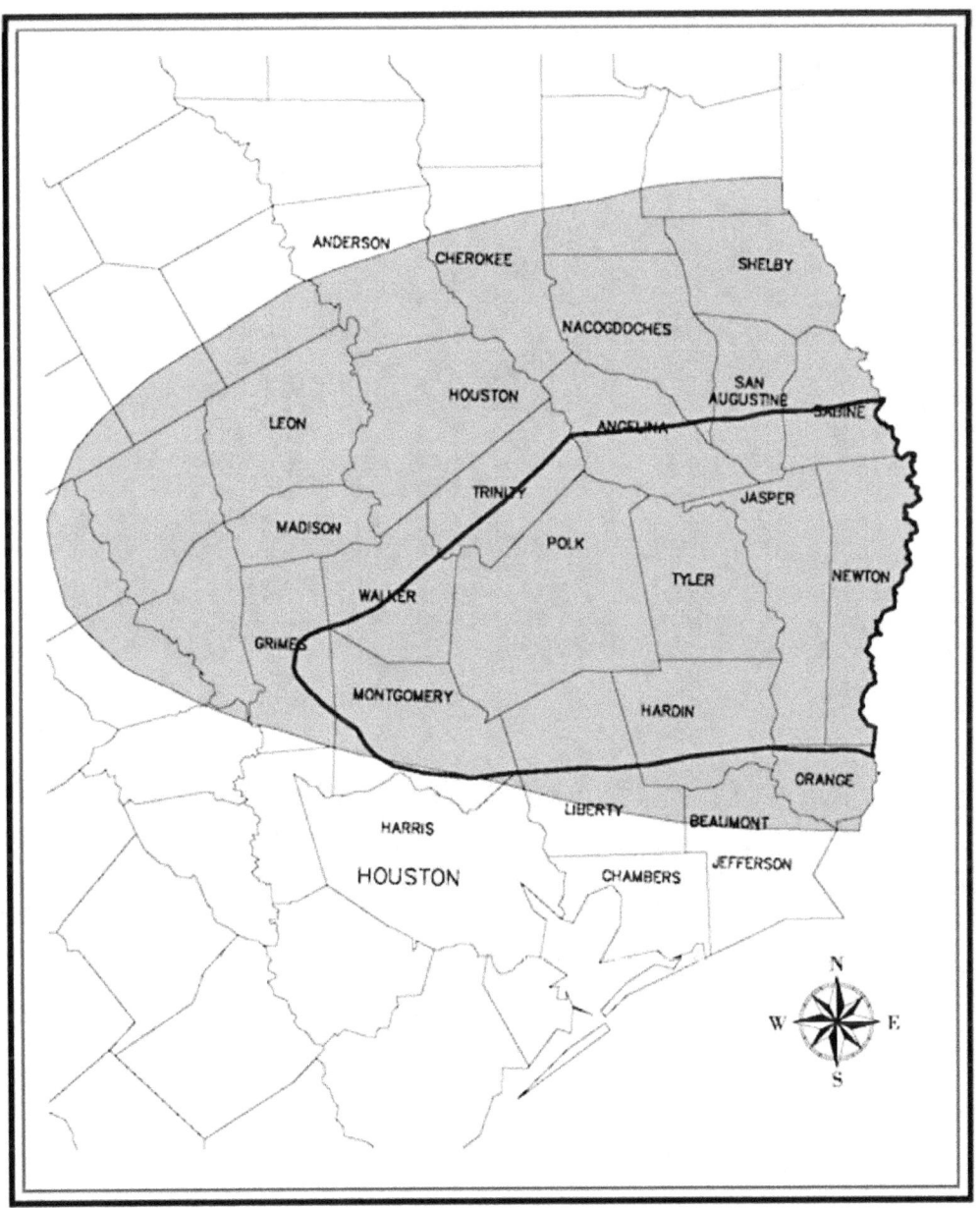

FIG. 2: GOVERNOR PRICE DANIELS PROPOSED
STATE PARK AREA AND THE 1936 BIOLOGICAL SURVEY

2. Small Scale Maps:

The Cartography of Disagreement

If it can be argued, as the 1936 Survey did, that the Big Thicket had great transverse width (more than 100 miles west to east), it is clear that most attention was paid, then and now, by conservationists and their adversaries to its central and not to its western or eastern reaches: a flaw of attention which, as noted above, continues to this day. It was important therefore that biologist Del Weniger, in researching the pioneer history of the western Big Thicket, was able to add significantly to our knowledge of the Big Thicket's western region, and, importantly, to describe its location. Weniger used accounts of pre-1860 Texas explorers to establish what plants, animals and landforms existed in different parts of the state prior to its massive transformation by settlers and railroad builders. His research showed that the western part of the Big Thicket region had been termed "Big Thicket" prior to the Civil War with portions already being cleared at that time. He concludes from the remarks of early explorers that it was

> ...a region of mostly large, dense timber with high, fertile, productive soil already with extensive settlement in 1858. The location is that known today as the Big Thicket.[3]

The map derived from Weniger's historical research is as follows:

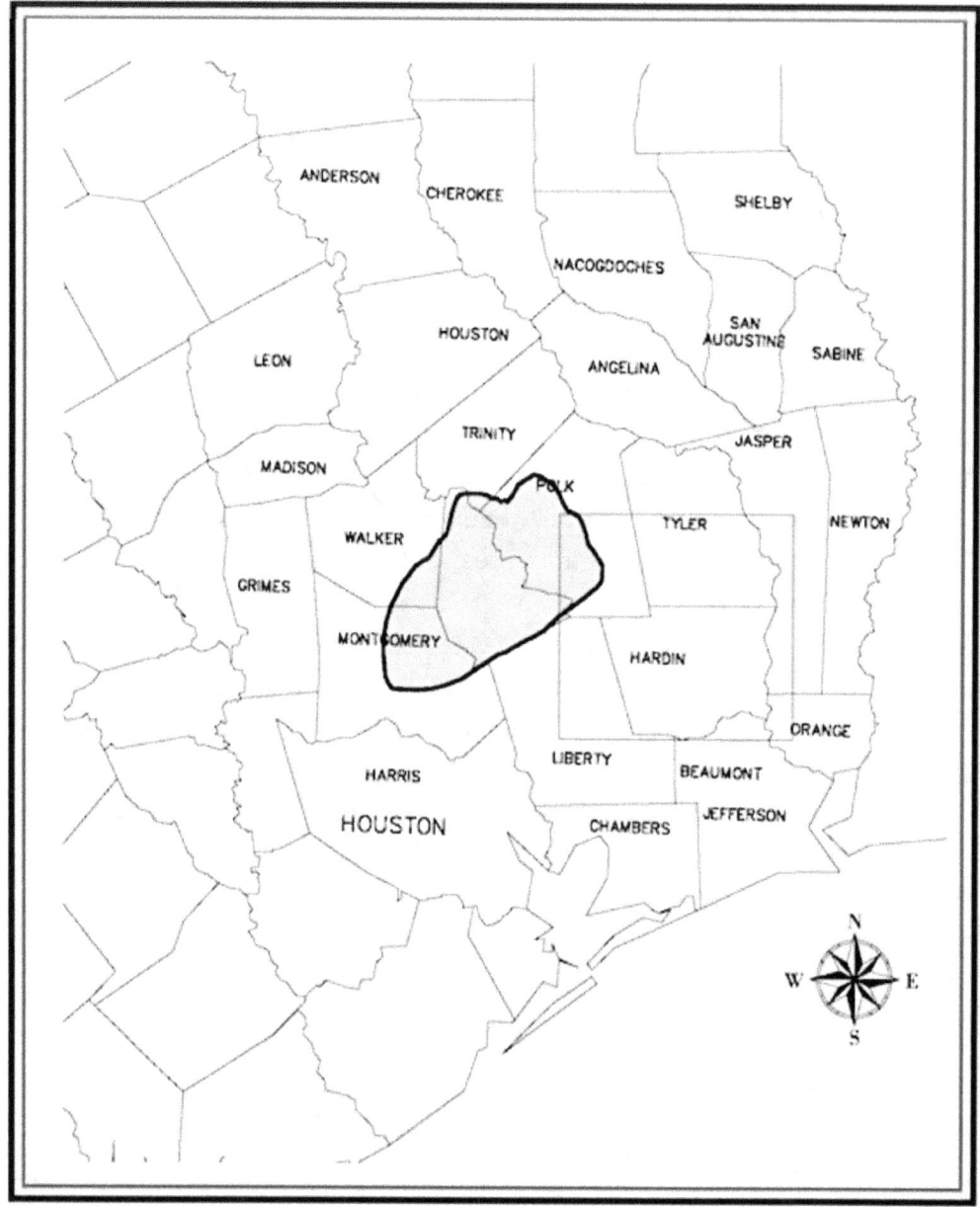

FIG. 3: WENIGER'S WESTERN BIG THICKET

Weniger, drawing entirely on historical factors and rejecting biology, concludes that the Big Thicket existed only in its western region, and only in parts of three counties: Montgomery, San Jacinto, and Polk. At best he held that some areas to the east of this area could be called "Thickety Country" and that the national park established there must be termed the Thickety Country National Park.[4] (The "park" he mentions is the Big Thicket National Preserve, established in 1974. The preserve will be discussed at the end of this article.)[5]

Weniger's denial of the existence of any Big Thicket except the area contained in his own map had already been countered by an equally dogmatic claim: that the "Thicket" existed only to the east of Weniger's Big Thicket and only in parts of Polk and Hardin Counties. The writer has been able to find two maps of this region. The first was proposed by the well-known folklorist F. E. Abernethy in his *Tales from the Big Thicket* (1966; rpt).

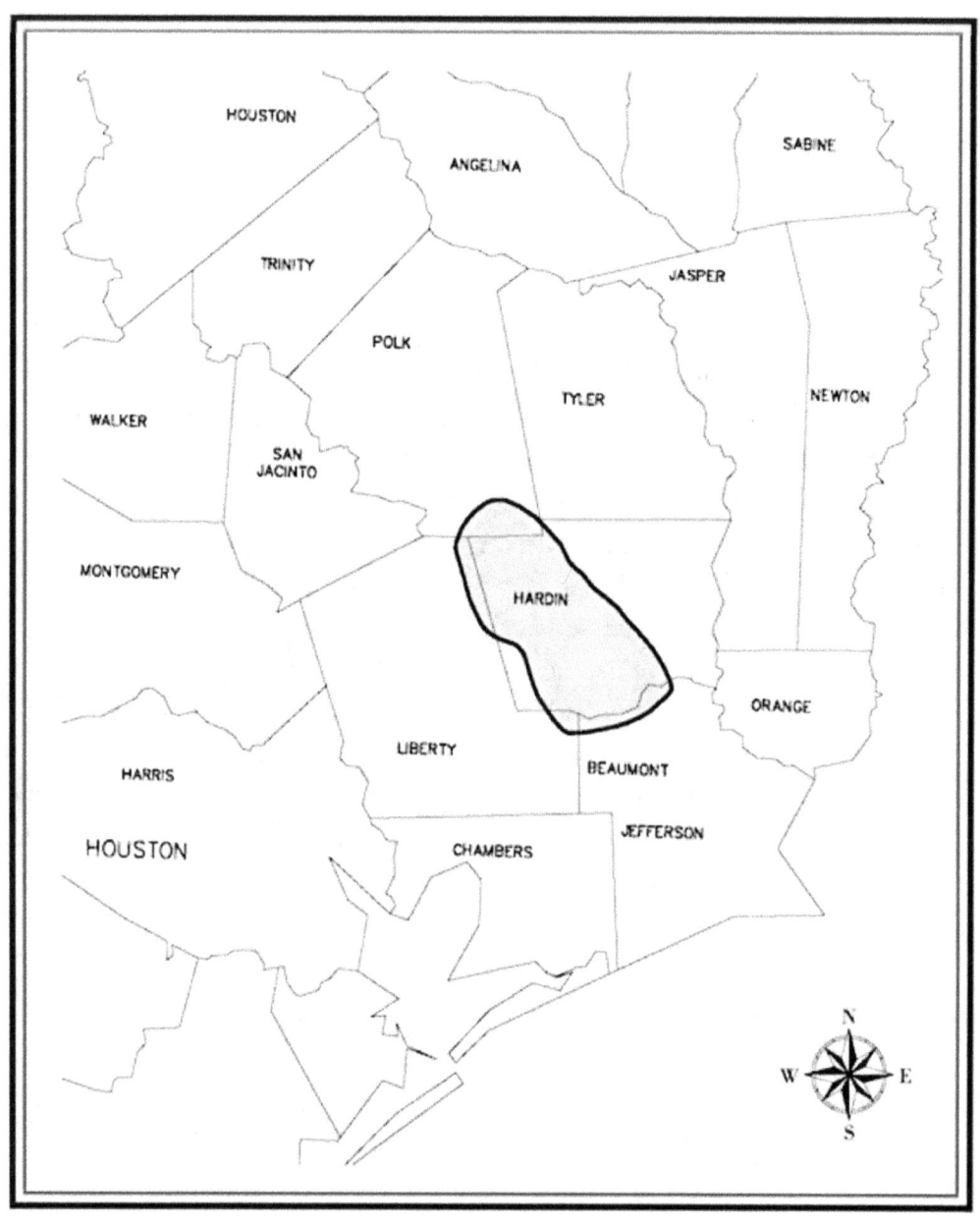

FIG. 4: ABERNETHY'S OLD BEAR HUNTER'S THICKET

By far the larger part of this map (well over ¾) lies within Hardin County.[6] The exceptions are a small area in the southeast corner of Polk County and two slender areas just within the boundaries of Liberty County to the west. Save for another sub-region on its east central side, this map of the Bear Hunters Thicket consists entirely of the swampy densely wooded Pine Island Bayou drainage basin, which empties into the Neches River just north of Beaumont.

While Abernethy's Big Thicket portrait is based, he insists, on general folklore, A. R. "Dolph" Fillingim's is derived from experience: his recollection of the boundaries of the Bear Hunter's Thicket when he was a young man, around 1910.

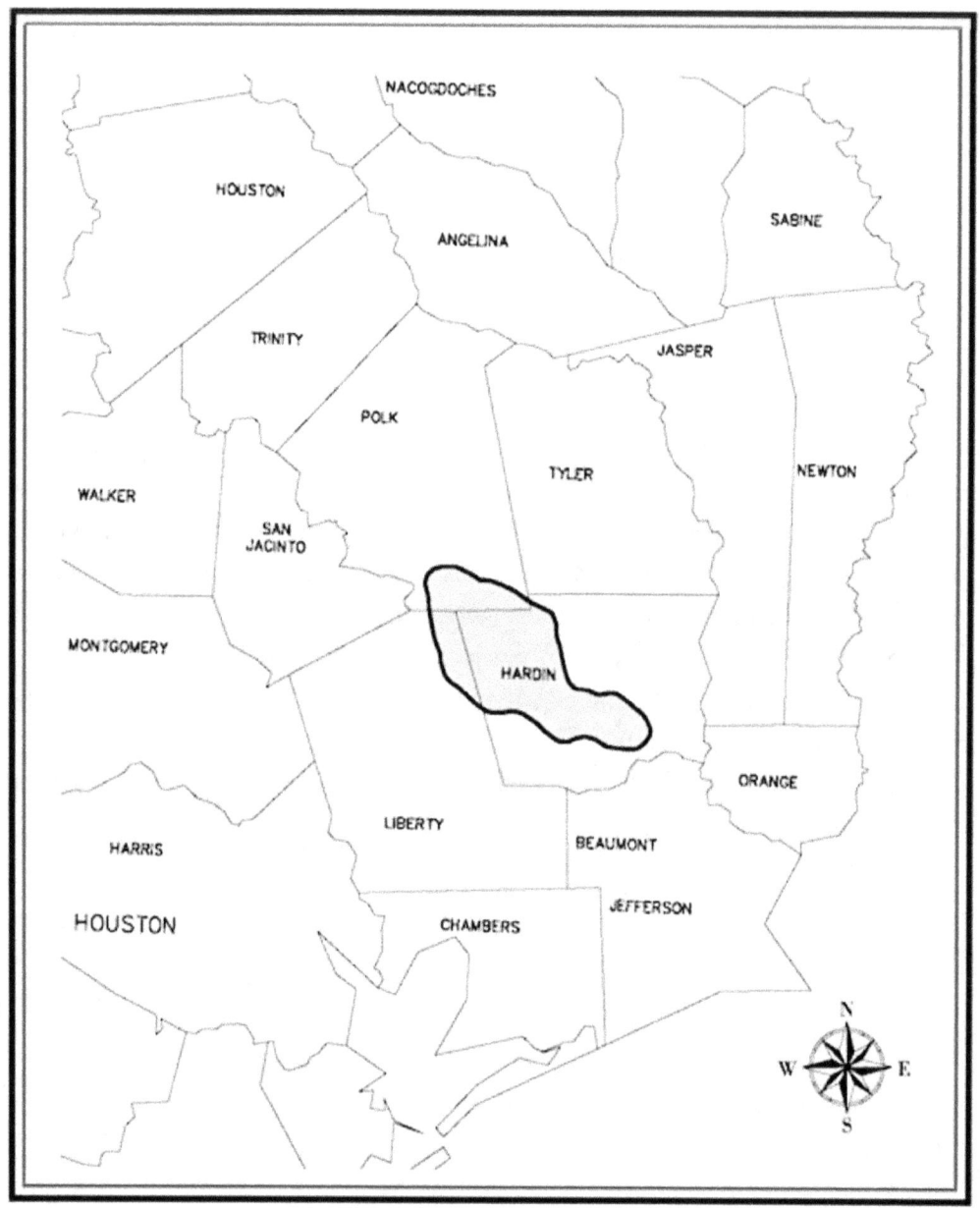

FIG. 5: DOLPH FILLINGIM'S OLD BEAR HUNTER'S THICKET

What follows is a composite of the two maps: a superposition of Fillingim's depiction with Abernethy's:[7]

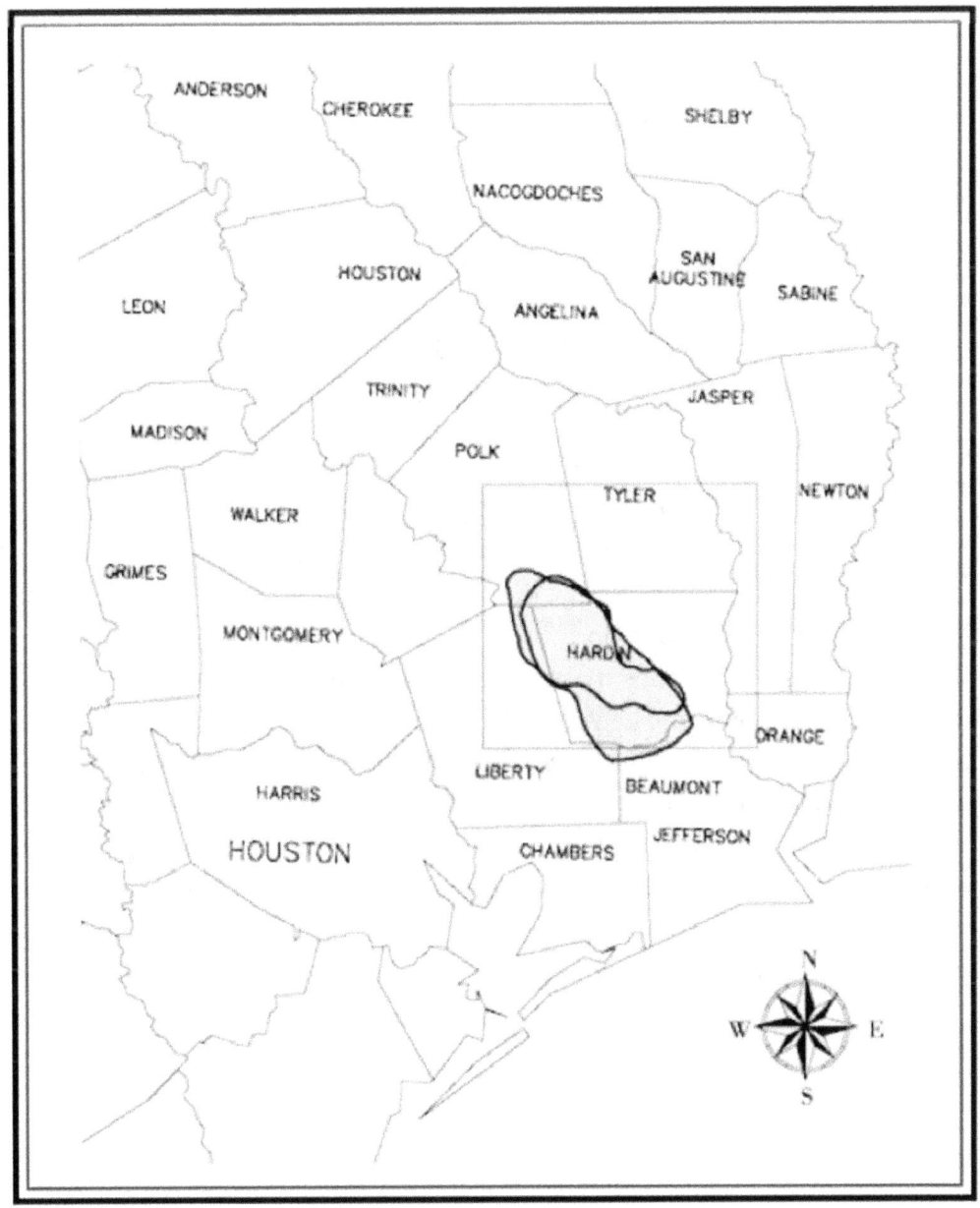

FIG. 6: AND FILLINGIM'S
OLD BEAR HUNTER'S THICKET

The most noticeable difference between these maps is that the southeast portion of the area singled out by Fillingim is considerably narrower than that claimed by Abernethy. By contrast, Fillingim's Hunter's Thicket extends farther north and farther northwest into the Trinity River basin in Liberty County.

Others have agreed with Abernethy and Fillingim about the centrality of the Bear Hunter's Thicket. Frederic W. Simonds, a geology professor at the University of Texas, locates the Big Thicket in a ten to fifteen mile wide area in the lower part of Hardin county.[8] Elmer H. Johnson, in his *The Natural Areas of Texas*, holds that the Big Thicket centers in the upper part of Hardin County.[9] No less a figure than John Henry Kirby, the state's leading forest industrialist, insisted that the "Thicket" existed only in Hardin County.[10]

Together these authorities make more than a solid case for the reality of the Bear Hunter's Big Thicket. The very substantiality of this region, however, creates a problem. Could there really be two Big Thickets; one to the west, the other to the east? Or even more unlikely, can we believe that one of them is the "true" Big Thicket while the other is an impostor—a pretender to the throne? Given the sameness of forest types, soils, and topography in both, the question loses all plausibility. Some other viewpoint must be possible which creates unity or coherence out of this opposition.

Fortunately, such a reconciling viewpoint is available. It involves the Big Thicket National Park of 435,000 acres, proposed in the 1930's by Senator Morris Sheppard (D-Tex).

FIG. 7: SHEPPARD'S PROPOSED BIG THICKET NATIONAL PARK

The National Park map is easy to draw. It consists of Polk County—the whole of the county: towns, villages, and all.[11]

When this map is joined with the two previous maps, a very interesting result emerges:

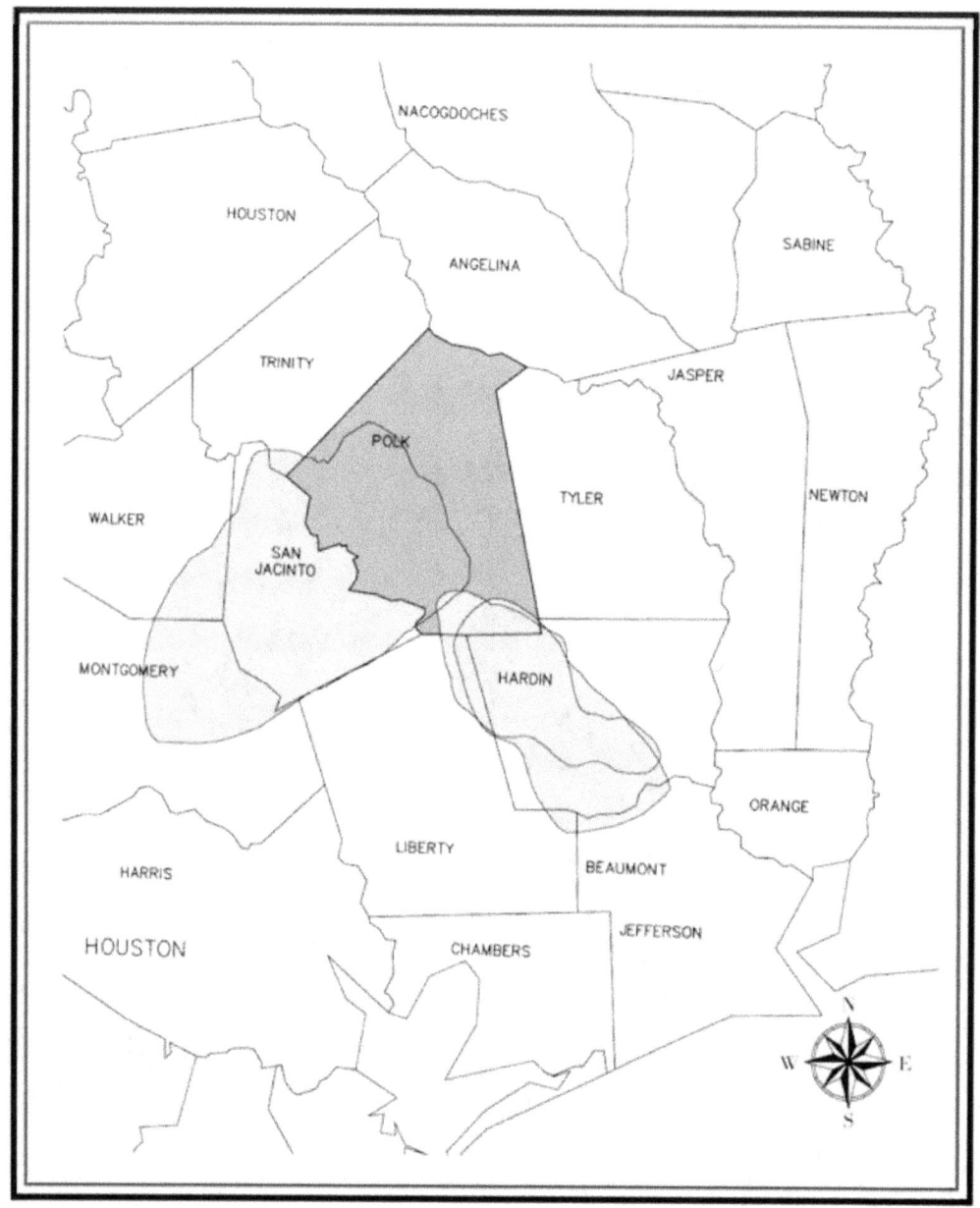

FIG. 8: ABERNETHY'S AND FILLINGIM'S OLD BEAR HUNTER'S
THICKETS SUPERIMPOSED ON WENIGER'S BIG THICKET AND
SHEPPARD'S PROPOSED NATIONAL PARK

Where before there were two separate, though in part overlapping regions, now there is one: a single region stretching from southwest of Conroe in Montgomery County and covering all of Polk and most of Hardin Counties. That is, this composite map portrays the unity of the western with most of the central Big Thicket. The two rival maps become parts of a single unbroken forest.

If this helps us to appreciate the existence as well as the character of the western and central Big Thicket, it leaves the question of the existence and nature of the eastern Big Thicket entirely open. Was there such a place? And if so, where was it? In part this question is solved through the examination of two further maps: one by J. Frank Dobie and the other by Benjamin Carroll Tharp.

3. Large Scale Maps:

The Cartography of Consensus

J. Frank Dobie is the acknowledged dean of Texas folklorists and a celebrated Texas historian. His brief description of the eastern Thicket is found in his *The Ben Lilly Legend* (1950). Here he states,

> The original Big Thicket of Texas lay for a hundred miles up and down the Sabine River with an average width of perhaps fifty miles.[12]

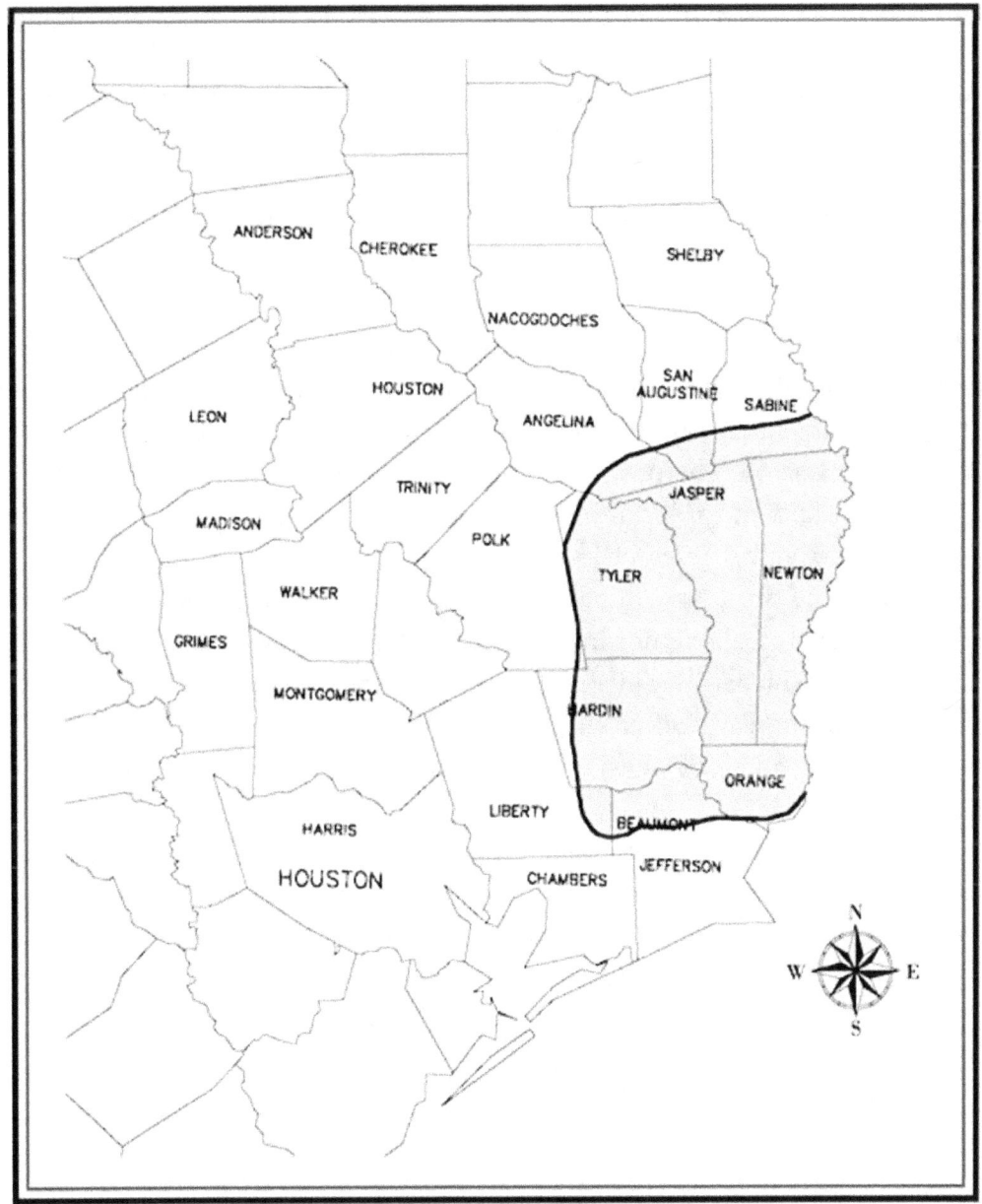

FIG. 9: J. FRANK DOBIE'S BIG THICKET (1950)

Dobie's one sentence map is unique among descriptions of the Big Thicket. All other large-scale maps present a general east-to-west orientation. By contrast, Dobie's orients the region north-to-south. Since he assigns no definite endpoints for his hundred-mile stretch along the Sabine River, the author will assign endpoints starting with Orange County's southern boundary and ending in Sabine county to the north. The western extent of his map is, following Dobie, presented as a mildly uneven line with endpoints rounded off. Here, as with Weniger, it has been necessary to transpose a verbal description into a cartographic structure. Point to point accuracy is not possible in such cases. The result of such transpositions, I argue, is largely accurate: representative.

Dobie's description is far from arbitrary. To a significant degree it coincides with the biological survey map. As will be shown below, it also shares much with both B. C. Tharp's map and the floristic map of Claude McLeod.

Benjamin Carroll Tharp, a botanist, has been termed "the father of Texas ecology." Best known for his *Structure of Texas Vegetation East of the 98th Meridian*,[13] he was a productive research scientist who contributed significantly to our knowledge of the plant growth regions of the state. It is interesting that neither in the book referred to above nor in his later *The Vegetation of Texas* (1939)[14] does he refer to the Big Thicket. But in an article in the 1952 *Handbook of Texas* (two years after the publication of Dobie's book), Tharp presents a map closely similar to Dobie's but with greater extension toward the west and a more broken, irregular configuration.[15]

Reaching west into Montgomery County and covering the southern half of Polk County, Tharp's map overlaps most of Weniger's western "Thicket"—but leaves out all of San Jacinto County, the center of Weniger's proposal. Including all of the Old Bear Hunter's Thicket, it reaches north along the Sabine River to include all of Sabine County: an inclusion which agrees with Dobie's map and which will take on particular significance when we come to compare it with Claude McLeod's floristic study.

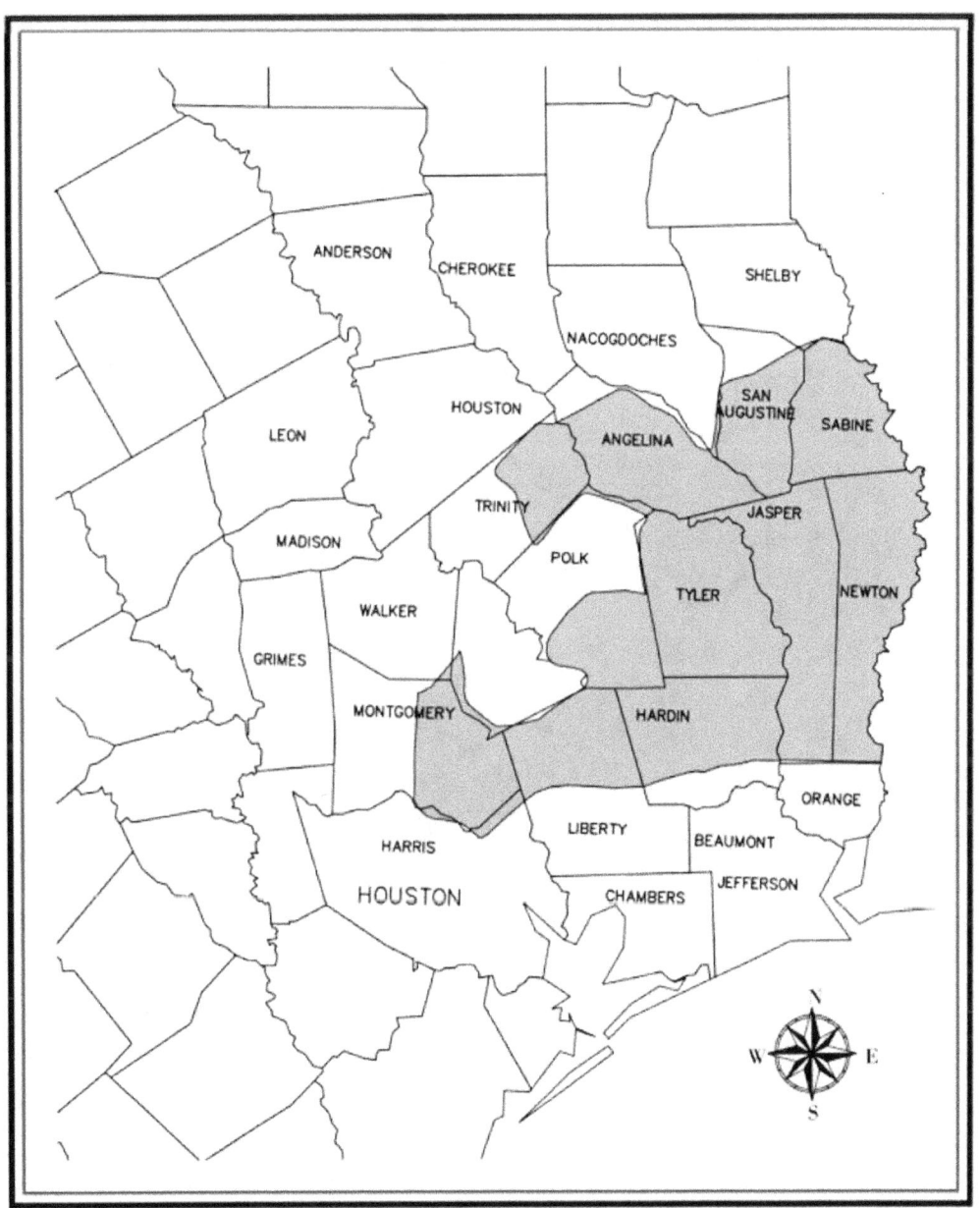

FIG. 10: B. C. THARP'S BIG THICKET

A composite of the Dobie and Tharp maps shows their essential agreement over the eastern reaches of the Big Thicket and a sharp disagreement concerning its western extent (Figure 11).

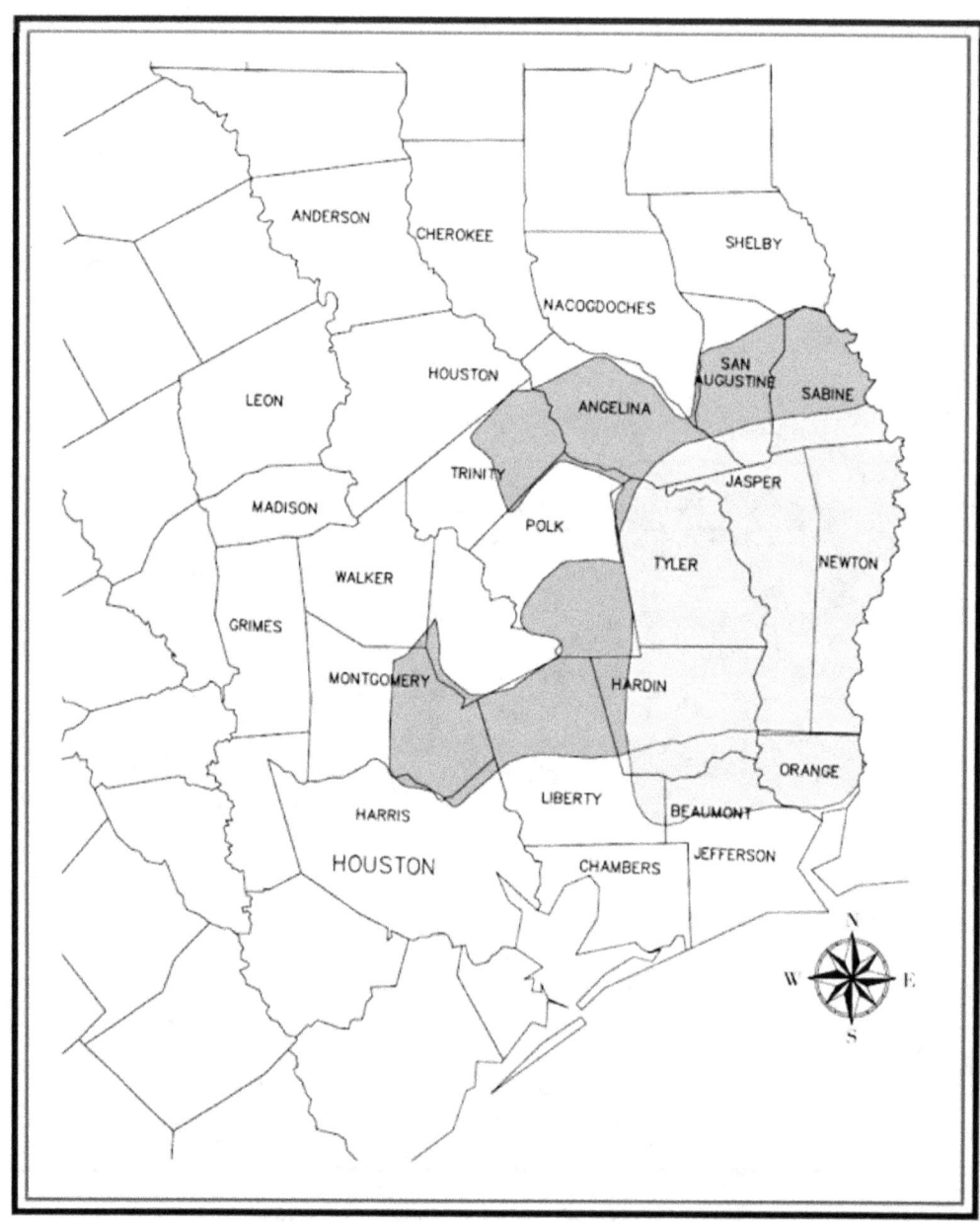

FIG. 11: DOBIE'S 1950 BIG THICKET
SUPERIMPOSED ON B. C. THARP'S MAP

It would be interesting to know whether or to what extent the two men's ideas may have influenced each other. Dobie used Tharp's understanding of Texas environment in writing several of his books, and the two men were colleagues at the University of Texas.

The author, having finished this comparison of Tharp's and Dobie's maps, still remains puzzled. Why should the eminent folklorist have positioned the "Thicket" as he did? For all his folksiness and his capacity to talk to a large, diverse audience, Dobie was a careful and painstaking scholar. He never formed his opinions easily.

The answer to this puzzle exists, I believe. It can be found in a book Dobie had edited in 1942, eight years before the publication of *The Ben Lilly Legend*, Solomon Alexander Wright's *My Rambles as East Texas Cowboy, Hunter, Fisherman, Tie-Cutter*.[16] Wright, who was raised in the Big Thicket along the Sabine River in Newton County, had a thorough knowledge of the region, having travelled widely, as he says, in "the Territory between the Big Thicket and Tarkington's Prairie," an area to the west, beyond the Trinity River in Liberty County.[17] When one reads his description of the Big Thicket one suddenly finds oneself confronted with Dobie's later description: slightly inverted or, rather, uninverted:

> There is a noted swamp country in southeast Texas called The Big Thicket. It extends across the lower ends of Newton and Jaspers Counties, down into Orange County and crosses Hardin, Liberty, Polk, Tyler and Montgomery counties. Before it was cut off and drained, the Big Thicket was maybe *fifty miles wide in places and a hundred miles long*.[18]

Here, in Solomon Wright's language, one finds all the terms of Dobie's map: a width of around fifty miles, a prolonged north-south extension along the Sabine River, and a length of one hundred miles towards the west. But in Dobie's one sentence description, the hundred miles is tilted northward while in Wright's the hundred mile length is positioned east-west. It is hard to escape the conclusion that Dobie's entirely understandable error obscures the fact that he had taken his later 1950 map of the Big Thicket from Wright's 1942 map, via a slip of the pen.

When this is corrected, one finds the following map, as proposed by Wright and (subsequently, minus confusions) seconded by Dobie:

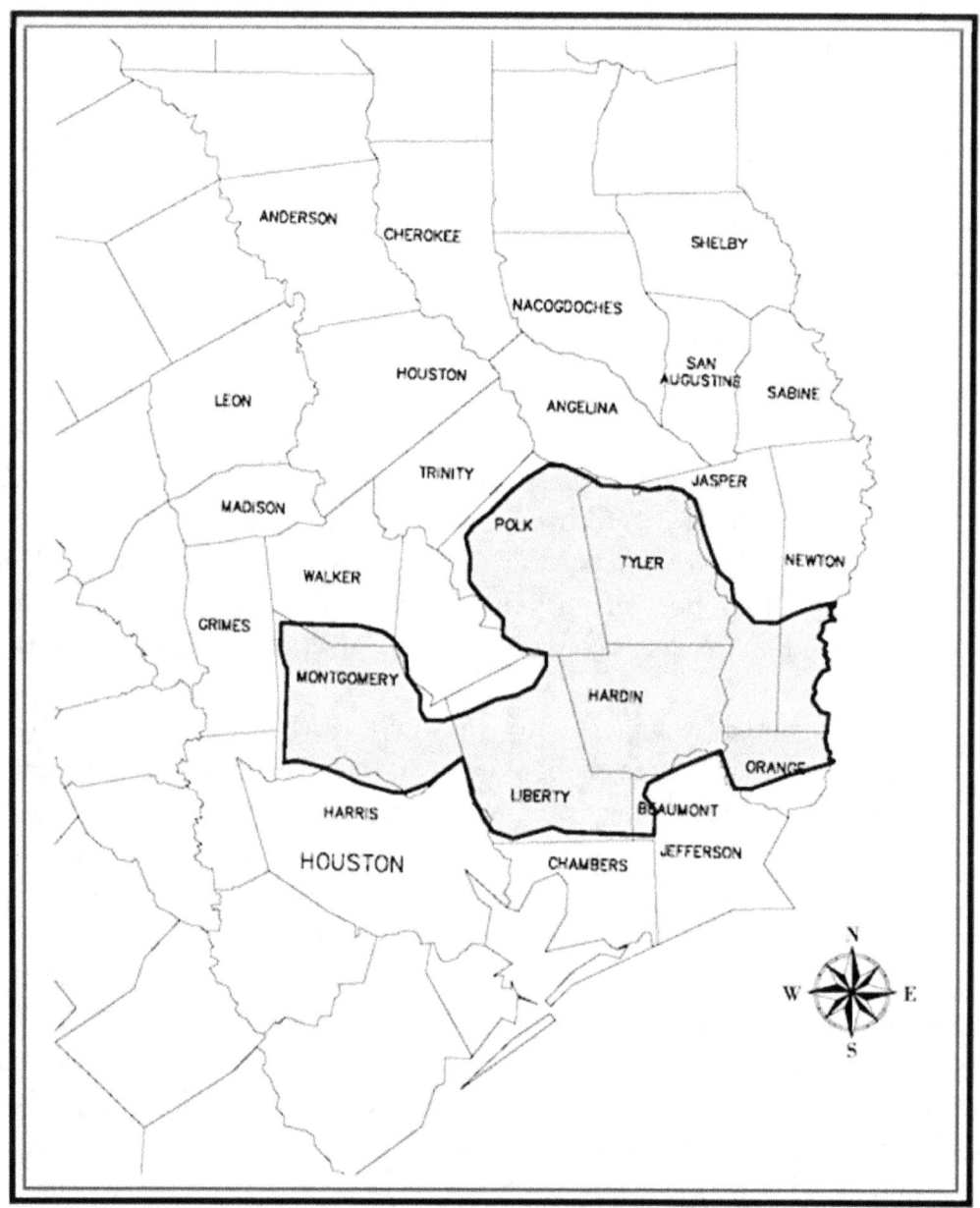

FIG. 12: SOLOMON WRIGHT'S BIG THICKET (1942)

When this map is juxtaposed with Tharp's, one finds close agreement.

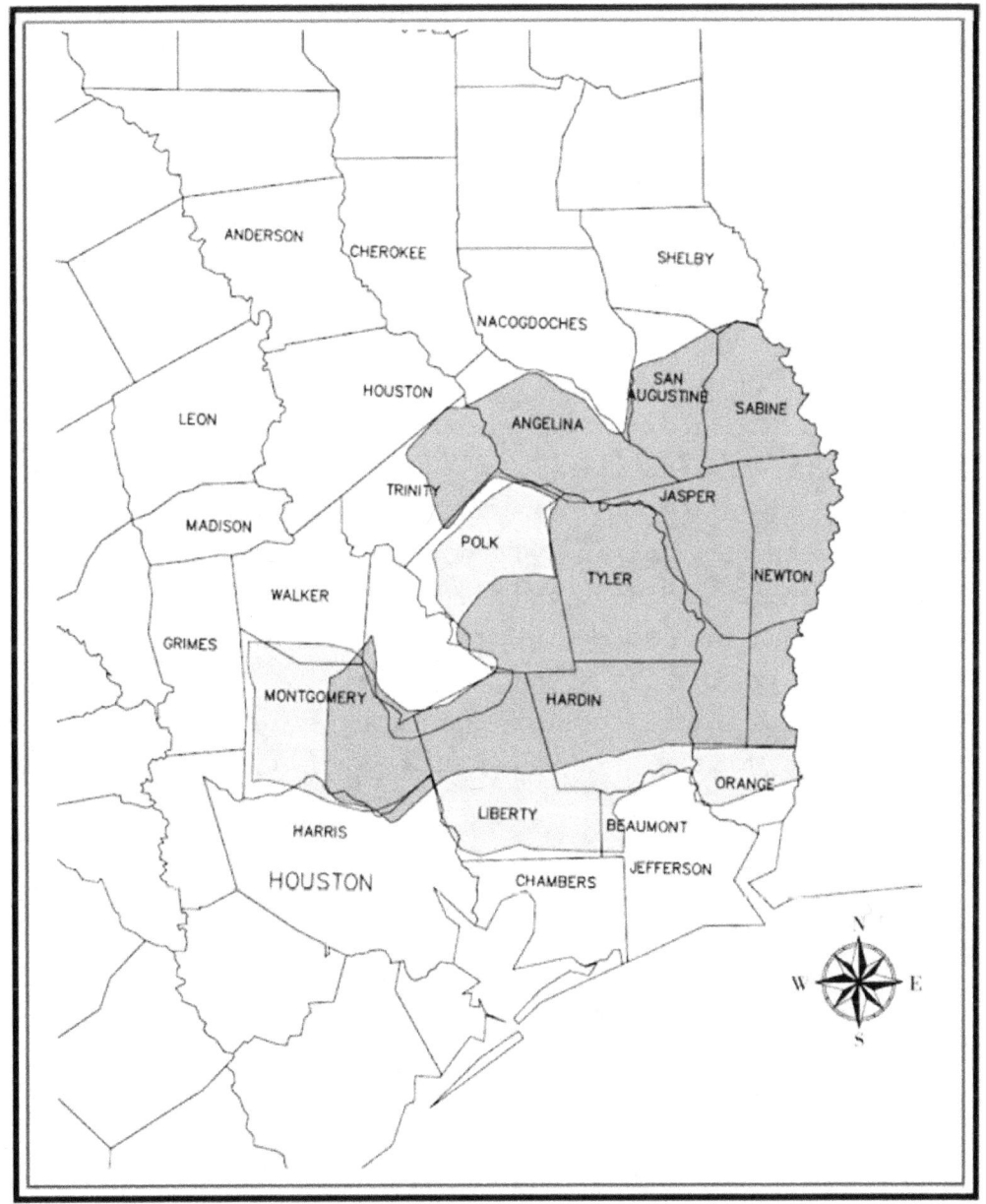

FIG. 13: SOLOMON WRIGHT'S BIG THICKET (1942)
SUPERIMPOSED ON B. C. THARP'S MAP

One now knows what J. Frank Dobie learned from Solomon Wright. It would be interesting to know whether Tharp, in turn, learned from Wright, or from Dobie. It is certainly plausible to argue, after all, that all three learned from the land.

Wright is important for his clear, definite mapping of the Big Thicket. But he is significant for two further reasons. First, his personal acquaintance with southeast Texas—from the Sabine River westward past the Trinity River on into Liberty County and beyond—provided him with an overview of the entire region. He had seen personally its western and its eastern parts. His inclusion of Montgomery and Liberty counties as parts of the "Thicket" thus cannot be ruled out as due to hearsay or current legend. Second, his confident inclusion of the land between the Neches and the Sabine Rivers as Big Thicket is equally telling. His family had come to Newton County in 1832 with a Spanish land grant. Their name for the land they lived in could not have come from later legends or newspaper reports. It was there from the beginning.

To Wright's map can be added an interesting and unexpected corroboration: the remarks of Vernon Bailey in his *Biological Survey of Texas* (1905).[19] In this survey, Bailey makes several mentions of the Big thicket, but most importantly, in describing a search for the swamp wood rat (*Neotoma floridana rubida* Bangs.) he states,

> The Big Thicket is a continuation of southern Louisiana swamp country, extending into Texas from the lower Sabine west to the San Jacinto (River) and marking the western limit of range of many species. Wood rats are well known to settlers throughout its extent.[20]

That he is personally familiar with many counties in this area is attested by his citations of many area towns, both to the west and to the east of the Trinity River. Here again one finds the prolonged east-west orientation portrayed by the Biological Survey, by Tharp, Dobie, and Wright.

4. A Summing Up:

A Convergence of Maps

The next step can be construed as a kind of grand finale: a bringing together of disparate maps to create a single configuration. That is, when the composite map of the western and central Big Thicket is conjoined to the composite map extending west from its eastern borders, the result is dramatic:

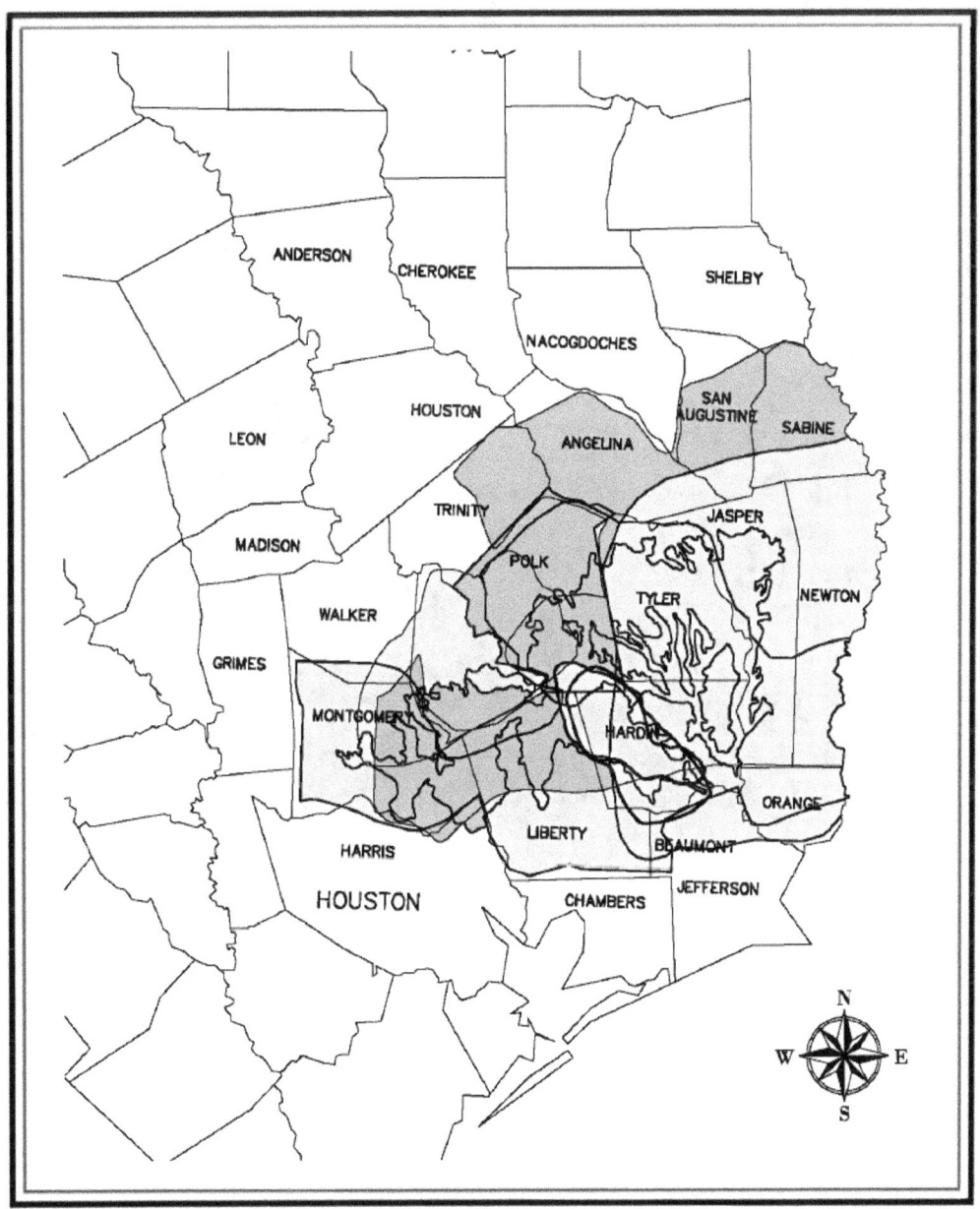

FIG. 14: ALL MAPS MINUS THE 1936 BIOLOGICAL SURVEY MAP

Here nine maps, arrived at by different authors at different times using contrasting methods and assumptions, become one. That is, they become single and, in spite of what might have been expected, in no way a loose aggregate. No areas are left outside these boundaries that might be termed satellite Big Thickets. Its boundaries are single, stretching in a solid line from the Sabine river to southwest of Conroe and east to the Sabine again.

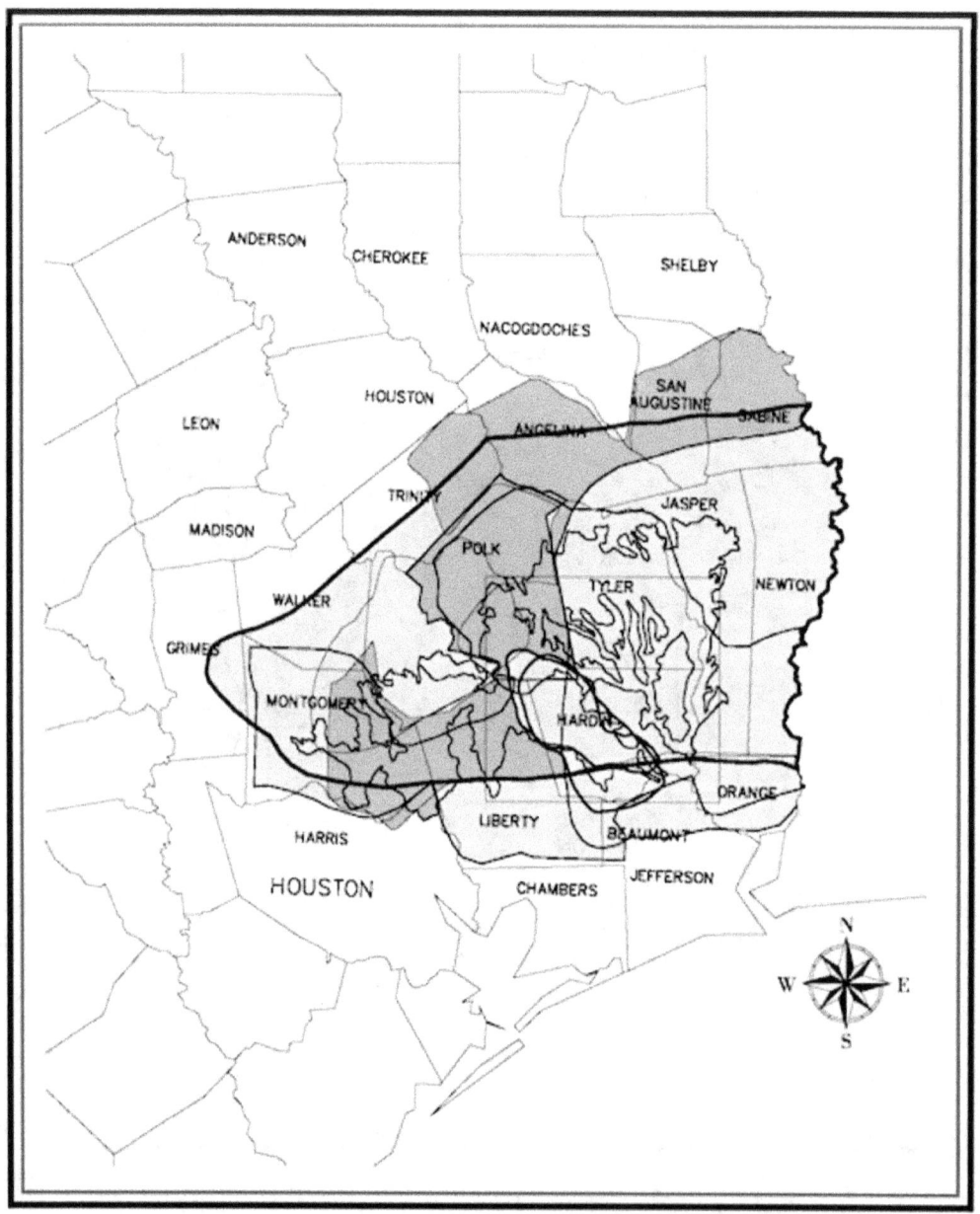

FIG. 15: ALL MAPS INCLUDING THE 1936 BIOLOGICAL SURVEY MAP

This geographical coherence is enhanced when it is compared with the 1936 biological survey map. Both maps depict a single contiguous area without gaps, and—again—without disjunct or "satellite" Big Thickets. Both maps cover essentially the same area.

The main differences in the coverage of the two are the exclusion of areas to the north and west in the large-scale composite map as well as the greater western extension of the 1936 survey map which includes (as the composite map does not) all of Walker, western Montgomery, and eastern Grimes Counties, the latter bordering the Brazos River. Both maps agree in having an extended north-south axis along the Sabine River. The southern borders of the two are virtually identical.

5. A Biologically-Based Map

The convergence of the various maps just presented provides a strong justification for the claim that in spite of the existence of conflicting accounts of its location and character, the Big Thicket consists of a single contiguous area whose outer borders (its perimeter) are generally agreed on by travelers, historians, and biologists alike. But one would like to know more. If the Big Thicket is one contiguous area, why do some areas within its borders (prairies, dry uplands, and others) not seem to belong to the Big Thicket at all? Why is there a dramatic contrast between the rolling uplands to the north and the low swamp jungles and winding bayous to the south? If the maps examined above show no breaks or "holes" in the "Thicket," then why do such holes exist? A more precise map of the area would help answer the question.

This map and this account exist. They are the work of Professor Claude A. McLeod of Sam Houston State University.[21] For those engaged in the struggle to create the Big Thicket National Preserve, his study at first came—for all of its detailed accuracy—as a letdown. If the 1936 survey had proclaimed an original 3,500,000 acre Big Thicket the size of the state of Connecticut. McLeod's map, by contrast, shrinks this primeval "Thicket" to 1,820,000 acres: a significant reduction. But McLeod's mastery of soils, streams, and plant communities and his painstaking attention to detail more than make up for this reduction in area. One observer, James Cozine, concluded that the very definiteness of McLeod's work provided the foundation in terms of which the Big Thicket could be "saved."[22]

In his first study, McLeod distinguishes a Big Thicket comprised of two distinct but contiguous regions. The upper or northern region is unified through a common "matrix vegetation", an over-story of loblolly pine (*Pinus taeda*), southern magnolia (*Magnolia grandiflora*), and beech (*Fagus grandifolia*). The lower or southern region continues the matrix vegetation of the upper Thicket, but lacks beech trees. Swamp chestnut oak (*Quercus michauxii Nutt*) takes their place. McLeod traces the complex structures of this matrix vegetation (a slope forest) along its stream corridors and areas of continuous woods. The result is a triumph of detail:

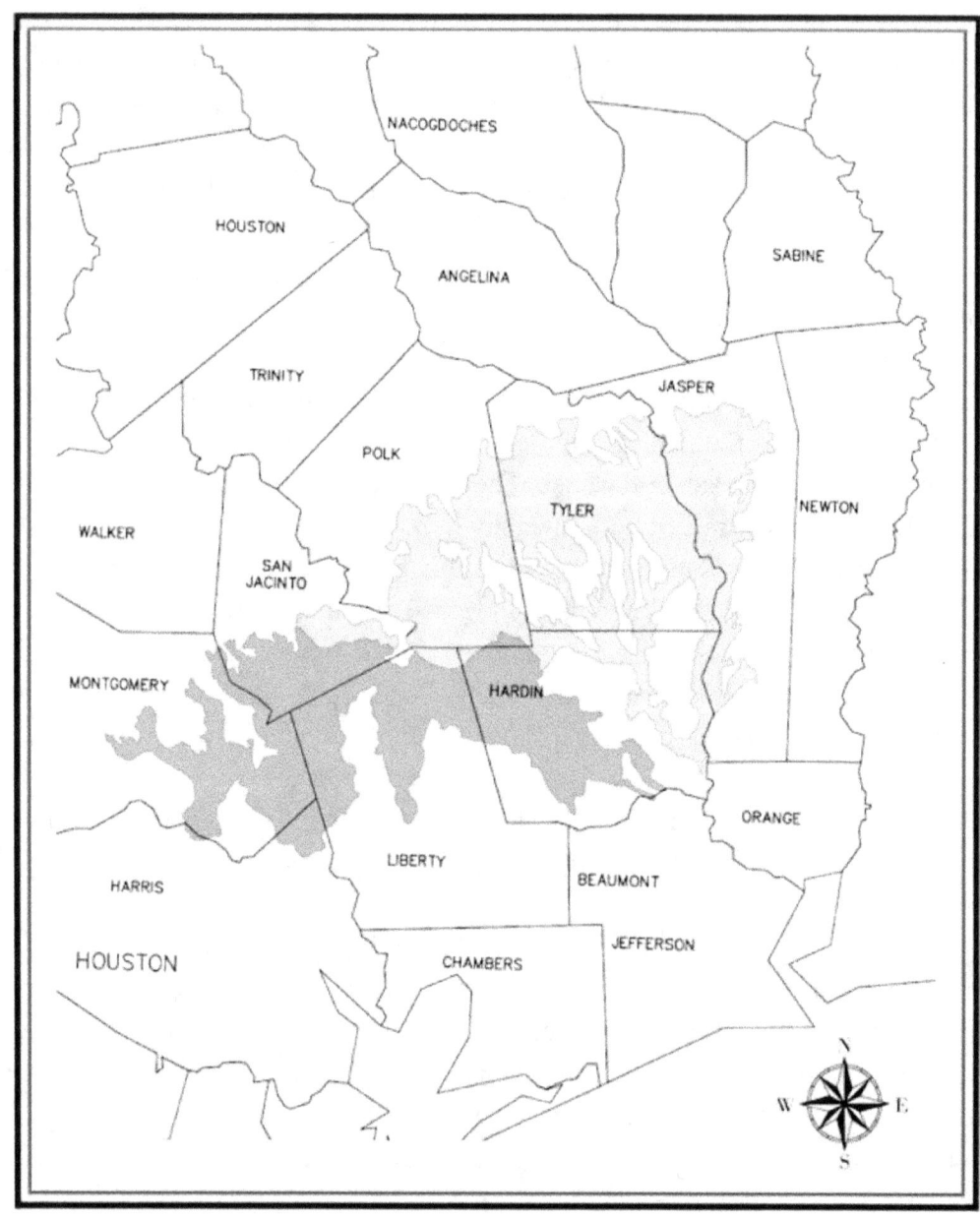

*FIG. 16: CLAUDE A. MCCLEOD'S ORIGINAL
BIOLOGICAL SURVEY MAP*

Some years later, McLeod added a further area to the Big Thicket: in Jasper, Newton, and Sabine Counties, to the east. The creeks and their tributaries in this region empty into the Sabine River. McLeod terms this complex the "stream Thicket." Here along clear, spring-fed creeks soils of sufficient depth and richness have been developed to support the vegetation of the upper Big Thicket. Loblolly pine, magnolia, and beech predominate, protecting a typically diverse understory (Figure 17).

Two significant factors stand out in McLeod's panorama. The first is its continuity. Though his stream Thicket contains watercourses which flow only into the Sabine River, the divide between the Sabine and the Neches River drainage basins is not sharp. In northern Jasper County, the two areas meet, making it possible to travel through McLeod's matrix vegetation from west of Conroe (on Interstate 45) all the way to the Louisiana border (well over 100 miles) without a break.

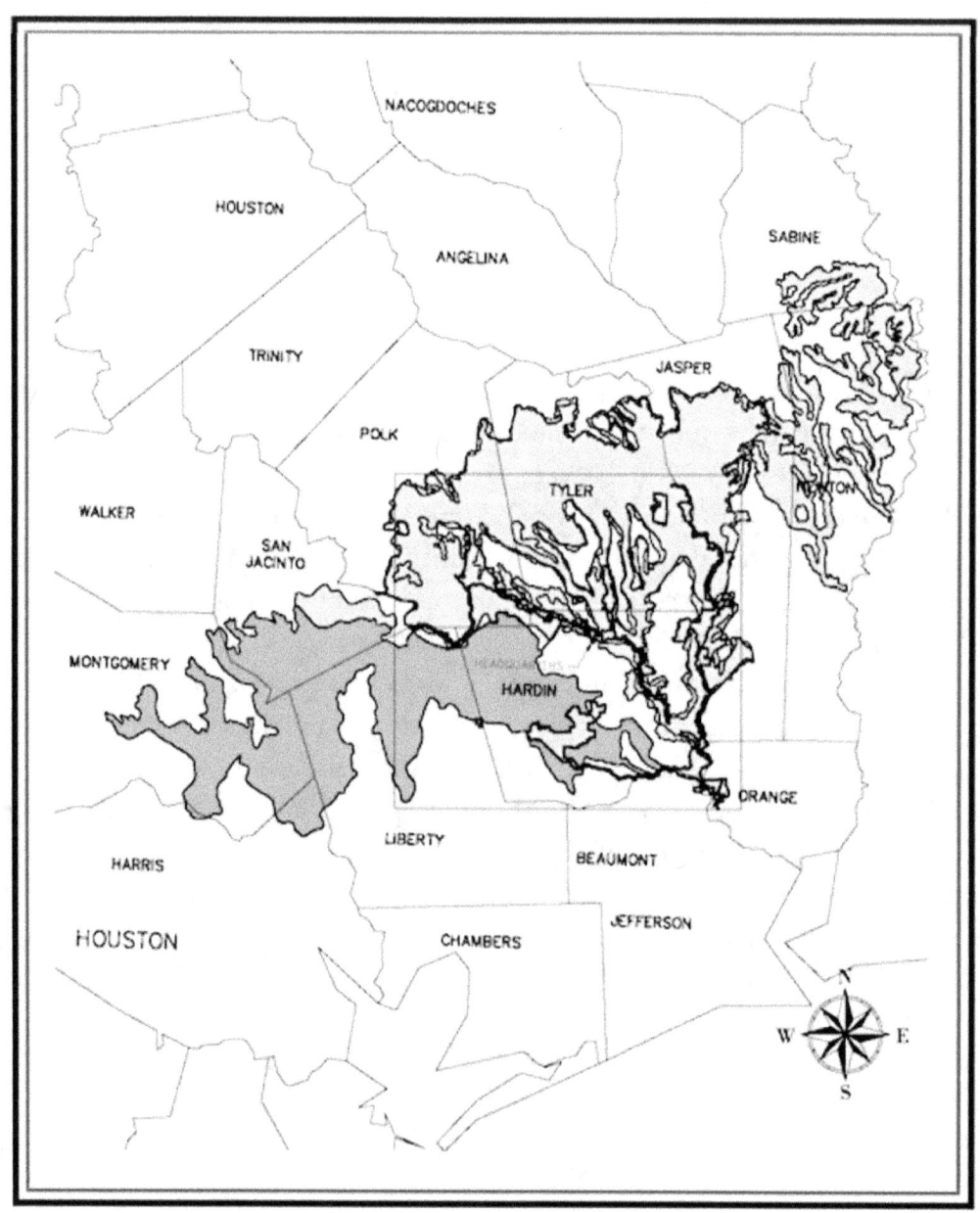

FIG. 17: CLAUDE A. MCCLEOD'S AMENDED
BIOLOGICAL SURVEY MAP WITH 'STREAM THICKET'

The inclusion of the stream Thicket also has the virtue of bringing McLeod's map in line with the other three large-scale maps of the region. That is, though McLeod's picture of the eastern Big Thicket does not trace its border along the Sabine River as far south as either Dobie or Tharp (or for that matter, the 1936 biological survey), it includes, like the other three large maps, a significant portion of Newton and Sabine Counties fronting the Sabine River.

The second striking difference between McLeod's map and all others, large or small, is the presence of holes or gaps in its continuous fabric. These, he explains, are the result of differing local conditions:

> Intrusions of the coastal prairie soils, more sterile longleaf pine soils, and dry red-clay sandy soils supporting short leaf pine-hardwood types tend to interrupt the distribution of the Thicket vegetation.[23]

That is, if we find prairies, longleaf pine savannahs, or shortleaf pine uplands in the Big Thicket, these islands of intrusive vegetation do not interrupt the continuous fabric of the "matrix vegetation" which constitutes the Thicket as a whole. Lumbering, land clearing, or other man-introduced procedures, as some environmentalists have held, have not caused these intrusions. They are, to quote McLeod, "long stabilized areas of habitat-vegetation relationships."

McLeod's standpoint is helpful in another respect. That is, it makes it possible to explain the many, sometimes conflicting accounts of the Big Thicket given by settlers, explorers, and biologists. Not only, on his terms, are there gaps or "holes" in the otherwise continuous matrix vegetation, but these are of different kinds (to repeat: prairies, longleaf pine savannahs, shortleaf pine-hardwood range). The existence of islands of widely different plant growth communities and soils is consistent with over-all continuity and with a single continuous border.

It is now possible, at last, to bring this discussion to a provisional conclusion. That is, the over-all regional maps can now be superimposed. The result of this superposition is as follows:

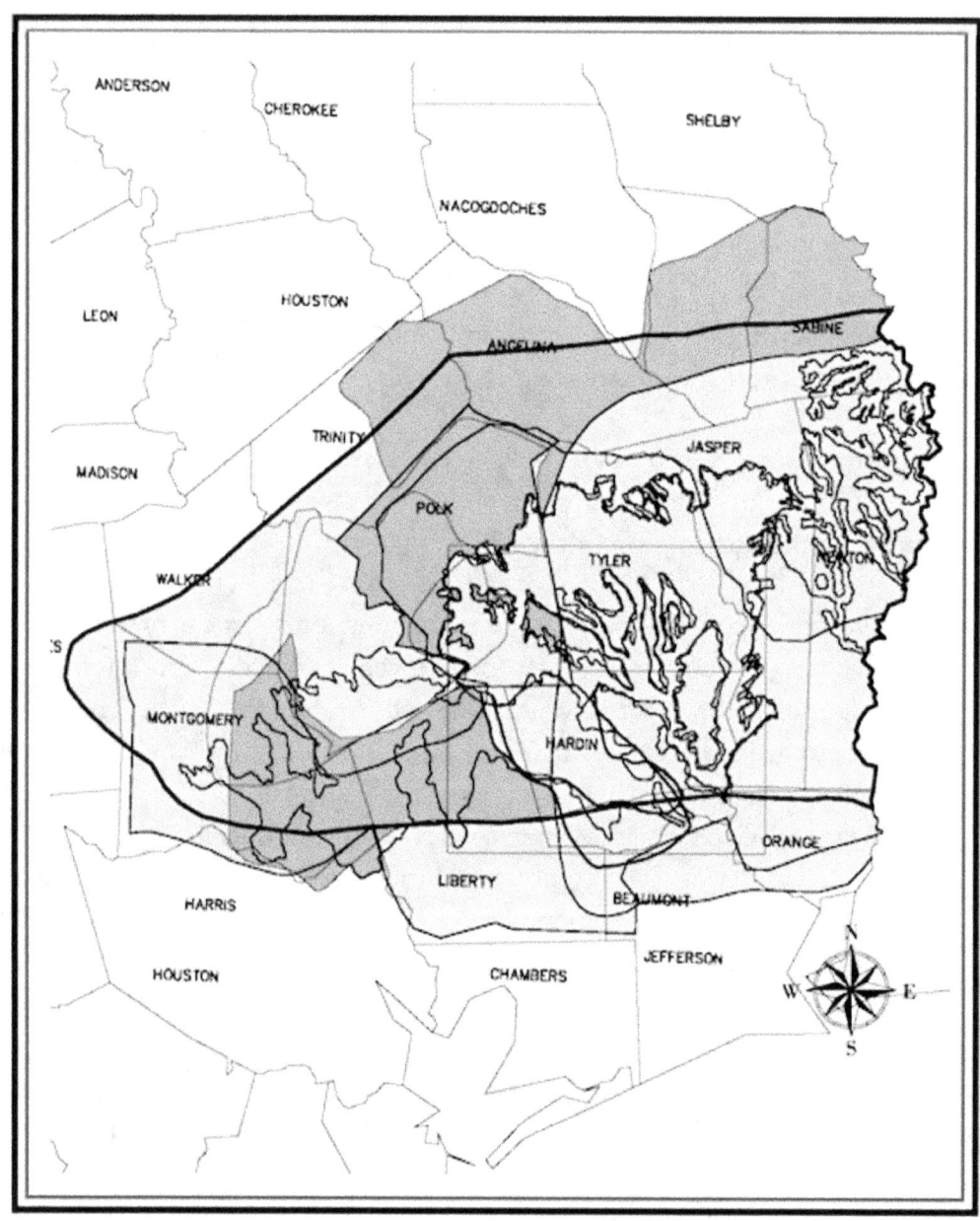

FIG. 18: ALL MAPS INCLUDING MCCLEOD'S
AMENDED BIOLOGICAL SURVEY MAP

The reader might well object that the map presented here as well as some previous maps in some ways look less like a map than a snarl of twine. But underlying the tangle of overlapping lines, curves and shaded areas lies a *fundamental identity*. As has been emphasized repeatedly in this article, the end result of a comparative cartographic approach has been to portray unity, not disagreement; cohesion rather than fragmentation. If the inclusive maps of the Big Thicket do not depict the same area acre by acre, their end result is, nonetheless, a clear convergence upon a particular region. It is hard to believe that this convergence could be an accident. Rather, it is a fundamental fact.

6. Folklore and Botany:

An Entente Cordiale

The reader has perhaps concluded from what has been said so far that essentially two different notions of the Big Thicket have competed for ascendancy over the years: first, the folklore depiction with its legends of outlaws, dangerous swamp forests, epic bear hunts and world-lost backwoods settlements and its proclivity for vague boundaries. Second, and by sharp contrast, scientific descriptions with their analyses of plant growth associations, soils, topography, species and subspecies. The competition and sometimes outright conflict between the two has left in its wake considerable confusion in the public mind over what the term Big Thicket can mean. The author can testify that it certainly complicated the decade long struggle to create the present Big Thicket National Biological Preserve.

What is that folklore—that vast-shadow of opinion without defined authorship or clear outlines—which more than a century after its birth, resolutely refuses to die? In the case of the Big Thicket, the folklore description is at least fourfold:

1. The existence of a vast, wild area sprawling west from the Louisiana border.
2. An area which deserves the term "Thicket": that, an area of dense vegetation, difficult, sometimes impossible to penetrate.
3. An area which, because of its density and remoteness, could serve as a refuge for fugitives of all colors and stripes.
4. An area whose shadowy remoteness forms the basis and the locale for unaccountably many folk tales (some with a kernel of truth).

Vastness is a relative term. The Taiga, the Sahara, the Kalahari are vast. To understand the Big Thicket as vast, however, it is necessary to think not of satellite views of massive earth forms but of days on horseback or river miles by canoe. By these measures, the Thicket would have seemed vast indeed to anyone attempting to travel there, particularly given the intricate twists and turns of its streams and the jungle tangles of their adjoining brush. In terms of distance understood in this way is it easy to understand its reputation as a "vast" area.

This reputation could not have arisen, or survived, the author insists, if the Big Thicket were, as some would have it, two or three counties in extent. Nor could it have persisted well beyond the bounds of the Lone Star State to the extent that it did. Its far-flung reputation is repeatedly stressed in *The Big Thicket*,[24] a little known but fascinating novel by Edmund E. Talbot of New Orleans. Using his Louisiana family background and his knowledge of general history, Talbot describes the trials of a poor Mississippi hill farmer who deserts the Confederate Army and seeks refuge in Texas' Big Thicket. Talbot's novel, written in the 1930's, provides an engrossing picture of the Civil War in the trans-Mississippi South. Repeatedly he depicts the Thicket as "the destination of all refugees"[25] where people from as far away Georgia trek to escape the travails of the crumbling Confederacy.

Besides its status as a refugee for men who, in J. Frank Dobie's words "wanted to forget and be forgotten,"[26] Big Thicket folklore also raises a second question: The notion of the region as a Thicket, a single dense impassable barrier. McLeod's researches clearly show, as noted above, that the region's prairies and open forests were real. Equally, his matrix vegetation—loblolly pines and magnolia—originally comprised an old growth forest which typically shaded out undergrowth. Such areas were open roads for men on foot or horseback, though the sheer massiveness of some trees in many of these forests would have made wagon travel difficult, and in some places impossible. But the Big Thicket also was and is a place—a network—of streams, large and small, whose corridors and banks, to make the point again, support dense, jungle-like vegetation. The sheer multiplicity of interlocking watercourses would by themselves have made travel hard going. The adjoining dense brush would often have rendered it impossible. Tharp states the situation clearly:

> Much of the ground water was returned to the surface in seepy areas along the slopes, in the 'bay galls' or through extensive swampy areas in the flood plains of the creeks... Those swampy areas in addition to being impassable themselves by reason of their miry nature, supported a growth of large and small hardwood vegetation so dense as to merit the name thicket. Since these thickets occupied an intricate network over the whole area it was impossible for a traveller to proceed far without encountering one.[27]

It is hardly surprising, in the light of this pervasive stream-jungle network, that the idea grew up that the region constituted a single thicket.

In one respect then, folklore surrounding the Big Thicket was mistaken while in another, involving the same characteristics, it was accurate. The legendary picture of the region as a single dense jungle-like forest goes wide of the mark. It was always a mix—a checkerboard—of openness and sheer closure. The legend of its impassability, however, was anything but a fiction. Stream web works choked with retinues of profuse jungle-like growth made travel there hard and often impossible. In this respect, folklore was on the mark. For the intrepid traveller, the Thicket was a thicket.

Another piece of folklore, beyond that of the extent and remoteness of the Big Thicket and its consequent status as a refuge, is the legend of the region as a cornucopia or treasure trove of gigantic trees, ready for harvest. Professor Weniger, here as so often in his writings, strongly objects. The lumbermen's and settlers' stories of sizeable areas of massive trees, he argues, must be rejected outright. This is true because some accounts by pre-1860 explorers in the Thicket describe not merely ordinary pine timber in the region but areas of deformed and stunted timber.

A response to Weniger's contentions would involve a careful study of the records (most still extant) of early timbering and lumber mill operations in the region. The author is, however, able to provide some interesting insights into the size of the original Big Thicket trees, insights which aid in rebutting Weniger's denials.

Dolph Fillingim, in producing his map of the Old Bear Hunter's Thicket describes pine trees there, each of which could produce "a four or five room house, foundation, framing, walls, flooring, everything…".[28] Such giants, each of which could produce 2,500 board feet of timber, were scattered about the Thicket. Why were there not more of these? Why (another way of putting the same question) was the pine forest of Fillingim's time, and except for the giant pines, a forest of small pines, on the average 25 to 30 years old? Fillingim is able to answer this question. He cites reports by families who came to that area in

1860 of a forest containing massive pine, oak, gum and magnolia which had been felled around 1880 by a hurricane, leaving a mass of tangled tree trunks and limbs in its wake. By the time the Fillingims arrived there (1905), the tangle had subsided, a new-growth forest had emerged in its place. The huge old pines to which Fillingim refers were survivors of the hurricane's destructive force.

H. B. Parks and V. L. Cory give a nearly identical description of the impact of tropical storms in the region. In times before history, they state, tropical storms

> ...have cut great lines through this area. Because of the wonderful adaptability of plant growth such scars are soon healed and records of these storms appear as peculiarly shaped ridges all running one direction. However, when the moss and leaves are removed, the ridge is found to be an immense log..."[29]

The new forest is a new and doubtless less well developed specimen of the old. But the old forest was a forest of massive trees.

At least two interesting things follow from these descriptions. One is that the forest, and even the forest type, one finds in an area may not be only a matter of topography or soils but also of the context of forest history. The other is that the huge "one house pines" that Fillingim describes were lucky survivors of a forest in which such massiveness would have been the rule, not the exception. There would have been vast areas of such forest giants.

7. Maps: Present, Future

In the present article, the various maps have represented the past and the present. This concluding section will deal with the present and its bearings on the future. To do so it will present a final composite map, one which juxtaposes McLeod's floristic map with a map of the Big Thick National Preserve, created in 1974 to protect specimens of each of the region's plant growth communities. The nature and structure of this preserve turn out, it will be argued, to be prophetic. They point to the future of conservation in the region.

Those who worked towards the creation of the Big Thicket National Preserve (henceforth, the Preserve) were confronted with a dilemma. In the late 1930's a national park of 435,000 acres had been feasible. In the 1970's, environmentalists found themselves confronted with an 84,500 acre limit—no larger area, given both political and environmental reality, could be set aside. The end result was a series of "units," each of which contained one or more of the plant growth communities common to the Thicket.[30] McLeod's pine-magnolia matrix was found in most of these units alongside swamps, bottomland forest, longleaf and shortleaf pine savannahs, and other communities. These units did not stand alone. They were bound together by two stream corridors, that of the Neches River and Pine Island Bayou, which joins the Neches north of Beaumont.[31] To this, the Village Creek-Big Sandy Creek corridor was later added.[32]

In retrospect it is clear that in creating the 84,500 acre preserve, necessity became the mother of an invention. The conservationists had saved a broad representation of the Big Thicket. But almost without realizing it, they had done something more. By joining together three major streams, they had "saved" the lower Neches drainage basin. Their web work of streams and nature preserves had systematically protected an entire segment of river system.

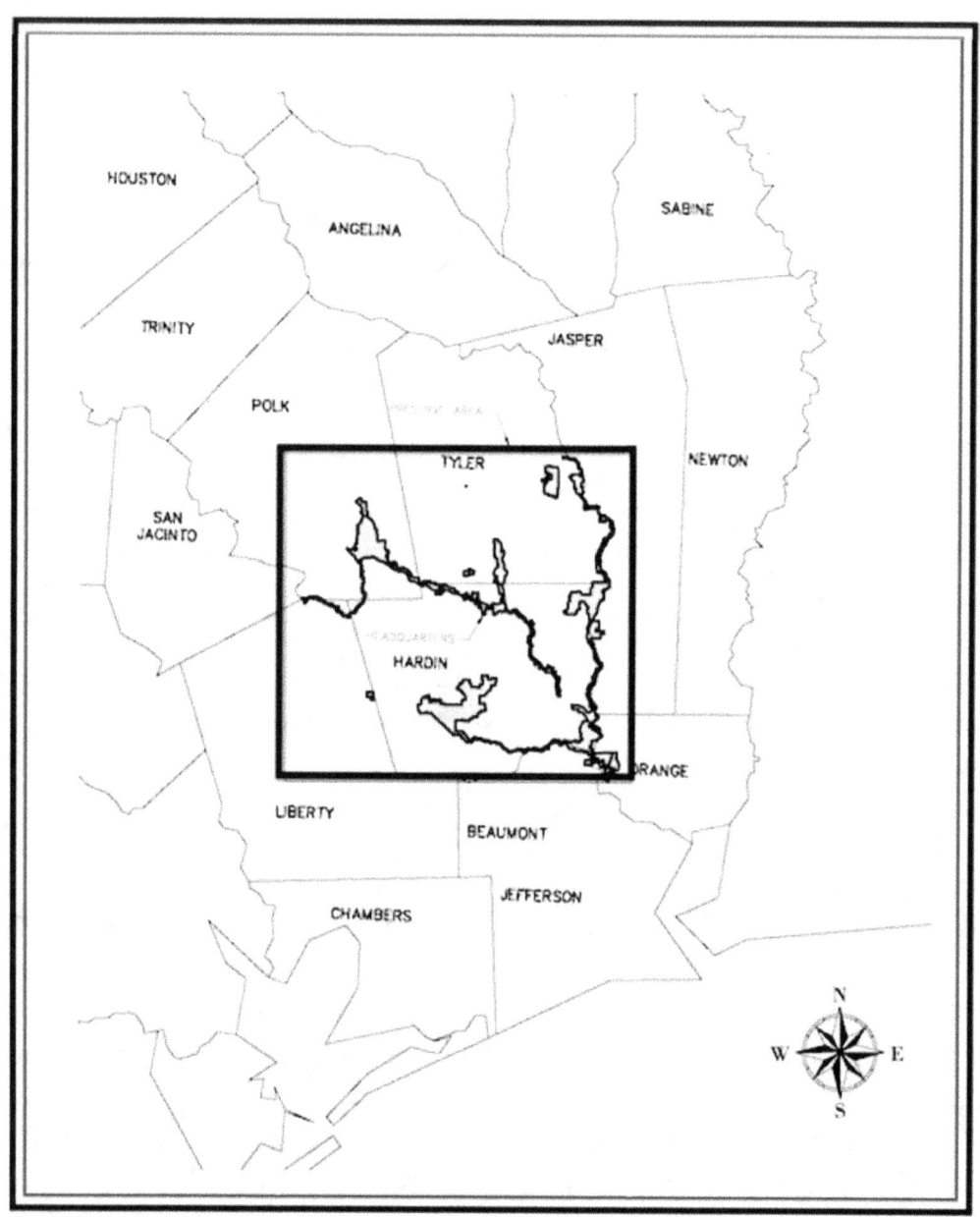

FIG. 19: THE BIG THICKET NATIONAL PRESERVE MAP

It is precisely because the Preserve selectively protects a drainage basin that it represents a new kind of conservation. The national park proposed in the late 1930's would have covered an entire county. The Preserve, by contrast, protects stream corridors and nature preserves, leaving large open spaces, making conservation possible in an area where development—of roads, subdivisions, strip malls—has already begun to take place. Such a pattern could be applied at many places where vast, wild expanses no longer exist, yet the preservation of natural values is still called for.

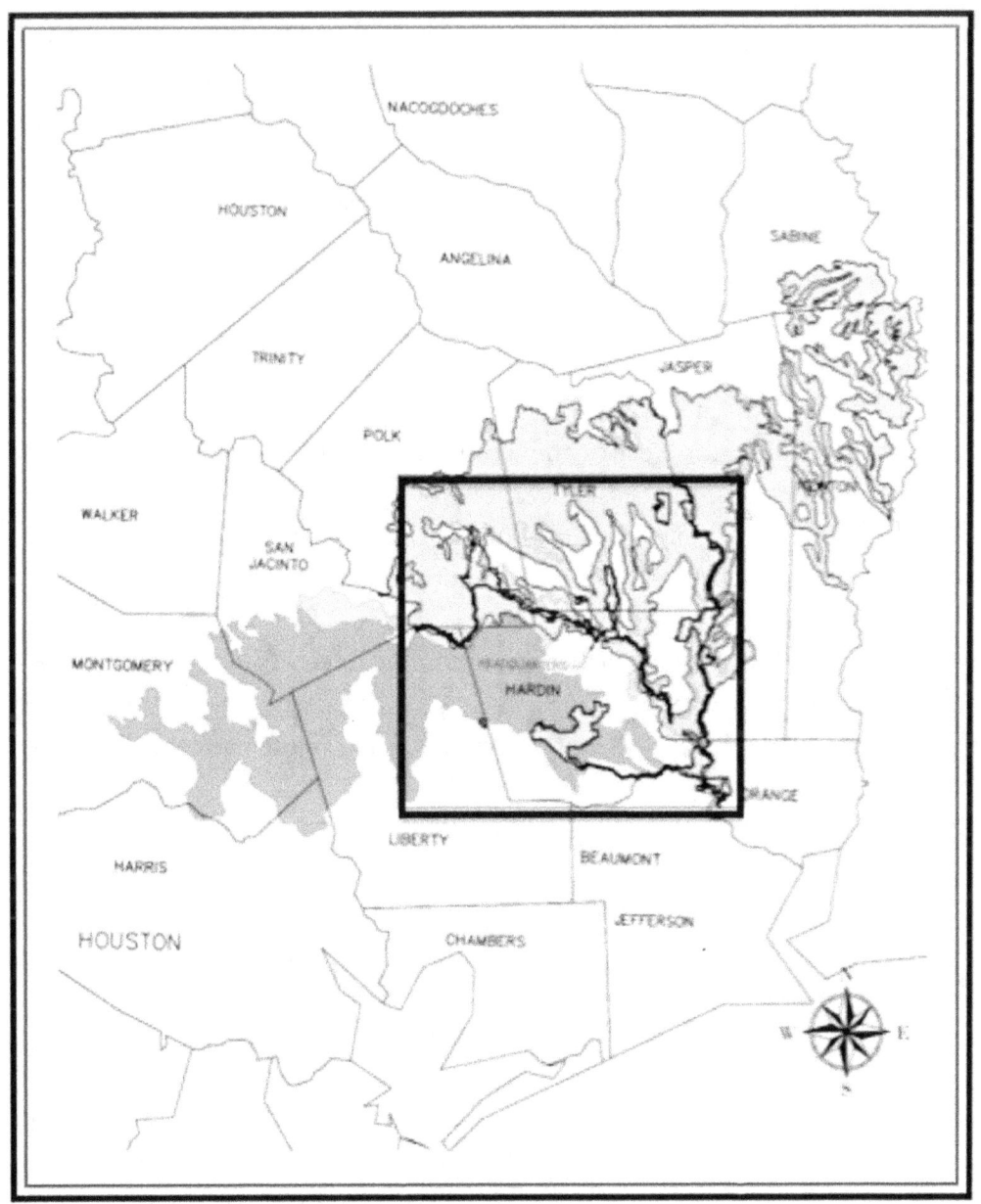

FIG. 20: THE BIG THICKET NATIONAL PRESERVE MAP
PLUS MCCLEOD'S SECOND BIOLOGICAL SURVEY MAP

The composite map immediately above suggests an important possibility. One reason lies in the centrality of the Preserve to the Big Thicket as a whole. Just as the Big Thicket National Preserve protects the lower Neches River drainage basin, but no more than this, so its many branches and related wild areas protect, so far as is possible, the central component of the Big Thicket, and no more. Both the eastern regions and the western regions of the Thicket are left out of the pattern. So are the still wild upper reaches of the Neches River. The Neches from Beaumont north to Dam B (Steinhagen Reservoir) is part of the Preserve and is protected. From there north, no such protection exists.

This situation opens up the possibility of both lateral and vertical extensions of the web-and-sanctuary concept developed in the Big Thicket National Preserve. To discuss these options in detail would require another article, at least as long as the present one. What follows will be brief.

Remaining wild lands west of the Trinity River from the Preserve and east of the Neches River, as this essay demonstrates, certainly merit the term Big Thicket. Yet conservationists have in the past paid scant attention to them. This, in spite of the fact that many areas draining into the San Jacinto River merit protection, thus saving remnants of the western Big Thicket, while the same can be said of McLeod's "stream thicket" fronting the Sabine River, to the east.

Several nature preserves do exist in the western Thicket: the Damuth Sanctuary, the Little Thicket Nature Sanctuary, the Winters Bayou Preserve, the Lake Houston State Park (now owned by the city of Houston), the Big Creek Scenic Area, among others.[33] These, taken together, contain approximately 7,848 acres. Other areas could be cited. But little has been done to connect these isolated nature preserves, and without stream connections the preserves remain orphans, isolated from each other and from the stream corridors which could connect them. It is interesting to note in this respect that in Montgomery and Harris Counties, the county commissioners have recently moved to protect Spring Creek (a tributary of the San Jacinto River) as a canoeing and hiking stream with parks and nature preserves along its boundaries. They thus repeat a process that already exists in the Big Thicket National Preserve, and they protect, I think without realizing it, a segment of the western Big Thicket.[34]

East of the Preserve is the same relative neglect one finds to the west. McLeod's stream Thicket, the north-south oriented Big Thicket of J. Frank Dobie and Solomon Wright, the Sabine River drainage basin generally: these have been left out of the conservationists' concerns as well as forgotten in their projects. Three exceptions are the Patroon Bayou Mitigation Bank in Sabine County and, in Newton County, the Caney Creek Nature Park, and the Siecke State Forest.[35] No serious attempt has been made (as, by contrast, in the case of Spring Creek in the western Big Thicket) to safeguard stream corridors or establish adjoining nature preserves. Often this can be done by setting up environmental corridors along streams or by buying land from willing sellers. The bogeyman of an Evil Government moving in to take peoples' homes and land is a bogeyman and nothing more.

North of the preserve a still larger and equally important possibility opens up: the prospect of creating a Neches National Wild and Scenic River.[36] This project would in a sense do nothing new. It would extend the system of nature sanctuaries and stream corridors already present in the national biological preserve north along the Neches River, from dam B (Steinhagen Lake) to Lake Palestine.

Aspects of a wild and scenic river are already in place along the upper Neches: a wilderness area north of Steinhagen Lake at the juncture of the Neches and Angelina rivers; two National Forests with river frontage; a national wildlife refuge; two large nature preserves currently managed by the Conservation Fund; several smaller nature preserves with river frontage. The national wild and scenic river would simply connect these dots. It is important to note again that no land would be taken in creating the National Wild and Scenic River. Land on the river might be sold or donated. Or, it could remain as is, part of a protected riverway. None would be condemned.[37]

References

[1] Election Flyer, Big Thicket Archive, Gray Library, Lamar University, Beaumont, Texas.

[2] H. B. Parks, V. L. Cory, and Others. *Biological Survey of the East Texas Big Thicket Area*. College Station, TX: Texas Agricultural Experiment Station and Others, 1936, 51. (2nd Edition, 1938.)

[3] Del Weniger. *The Explorers' Texas: The Lands and Waters*. Austin, TX: Eakin Press, 1984, 81. Weniger added a second volume to his Explorers series over a decade later: *The Explorers' Texas: The Animals They Found*. Austin, TX: Eakin Press, 1997, 200. (Subsequent projected volumes, unfortunately, were not published.)

[4] The Big Thicket National Biological Preserve was established in 1974, a decade before Weniger published his own research. Oddly, he makes no mention anywhere in his treatment of the Big Thicket of Claude McLeod's researches or of the Preserve.

[5] It is helpful to note an article, "The Big Thicket Ruins", in the May 03, 1856, *Texas Republican* that describes the ruins of an ancient civilization in the Big Thicket near Cleveland, Texas. While these ruins, remarkably, have never been found, the article describes the western component of the "Thicket" within the boundaries of Weniger's map and makes it clear that the term Big Thicket was widely used to apply to the general area.

[6] Francis E. Abernethy, Ed. *Tales From the Big Thicket*. Austin, TX: University of Texas Press, 1966, 244. The first reprinting of this item (University of North Texas, 2002) does not contain the map of the Bear Hunter's Thicket. It is reprinted, however, in Campbell and Lynn Loughmiller, Eds., *Big Thicket Legacy*. Denton, TX: University of North Texas Press, 1977, p. vii.)

[7] A. R. Fillingim, Robert Pierce, and W. G. Regier, Eds. *Buzzard Eggs and Other Big Thicket Recollections*. Kountze, Tx: Mayhaw Press, 1973, 21. Fillingim's map and discussion were originally published in the *Kountze News*.

[8] Frederic William Simonds. *The Geography of Texas, Physical and Political*. New York: Ginn and Company, 1914, 51-52. Simonds notes that he has been "guided" in his writing by Charles Mohr's *The Timber Pines of the Southern United States*. U. S. Department of Agriculture, Division of Forestry Bulletin no. 13, 1890, 42-48. But Simonds is not guided by Mohr; his description of the Big Thicket is a direct quote from him: "...the so-called Big Thicket in the lower part of Hardin County, said to be from 10 to 15 miles wide, either way" (46). The real question here, beyond that of some literary borrowing is, how did Mohr, an Alabama botanist, get his peculiarly limited concept of the Big Thicket?

[9] Elmer H. Johnson. *The Natural Areas of Texas*. Austin, Tx: The University of Texas, 1931, 148. (*The University of Texas Bulletin*, No. 3113; Bureau of Business Research: Research Monograph, No. 8.)

[10] James J. Cozine. *Saving the Big Thicket: From Exploration to Preservation, 1685-2003*. Foreword, Afterword, Bibliography by Pete A. Y. Gunter. Denton, Tx: Big Thicket Association, University of North Texas Press, 2004, 3. Also, John H. Kirby. "The Lumber Industry of Texas." In *The Encyclopedia of Texas*. Vol 1. Eds. Ellis A. Davis and Edwin H. Grobe. Dallas, Tx: Texas Development Bureau, 1926, 32. For completeness sake, one can add to this the trek of John A. Caplan through the Bear Hunters Thicket in 1887, published by J. Frank Dobie in Wright's *My Rambles*, 157-159. (Originally published in *Sunny South*, November 5, 1887.)

[11] *Biological Survey of the Big Thicket*, 4.

[12] J. Frank Dobie. *The Ben Lilly Legend*. Rpt. 1985. Austin, Tx: University of Texas Press, 1950, 104.

[13] Benjamin Carroll Tharp. *Structure of Texas Vegetation East of the 98th Meridian*. Austin: University of Texas, 1926, 100.

[14] Benjamin Carroll Tharp. *The Vegetation of Texas*. Houston, Tx: Anson Jones Press, 1939, 74.

[15] Benjamin Carroll Tharp. "Big Thicket" in *The Handbook of Texas*. Vol I. Austin, Tx: Texas State Historical Association, 1952, 160-161.

[16] Solomon Alexander Wright. *My Rambles as East Texas Cowboy, Hunter, Fisherman, Tie-Cutter*. Ed. with Intro. J. Frank Dobie. Austin, Tx: Texas Folklore Society, 1942, 159.

[17] Ibid, 64-65.

[18] Ibid, 61.

[19] Vernon Bailey. *Biological Survey of Texas*. Washington, D.C.: Government Printing Office, 1905, 163; 164; 91-192. (This study can also be found under the rubric U.S. Department of Agriculture Biological Survey, North American Fauna, No. 25.)

[20] Ibid, 107-108.

[21] Claude A. McLeod. *The Big Thicket Forest of East Texas: Its History, Location and Description*. Huntsville, Tx: Sam Houston Press, 1967, 33; cf. also Claude A. McLeod. "The Big Thicket Forest of East Texas." *Texas Journal of Science*, 23(2), 1971, 221-233.

[22] James A. Cozine. "Defining the Big Thicket: A Prelude to Preservation." *East Texas Historical* Journal, 32(2), 1993, 57-71.

[23] McLeod, *Op. cit.*, 13.

[24] Edmund E. Talbot. *The Big Thicket*. Austin, Tx: Little House Press, 1973, 98.

[25] *Ibid*, 81.

[26] Dobie, *Op. cit.*, 104.

[27] Tharp, *Handbook of Texas, Op. cit.*, 160-161.

[28] Fillingim, *Op. cit.*, 7.

[29] Parks, et al. *Op. cit.*, 10.

[30] For a description of the units and stream corridors of the Big Thicket National Biological Preserve cf. Pete A. Y. Gunter. The Big Thicket: An Ecological Reevaluation. Foreword by Bob Armstrong. Denton, Tx: University of North Texas Press, 1993, Chapter 6, 111-166.

[31] The exception to this rule is the Menard Creek Corridor and Watershed, which flow southwest from the Big Sandy Unit into the Trinity River.

[32] For a description of the addition of the Big Sandy-Village Creek corridor to the national preserve cf. Pete A. Y. Gunter. "Afterword" to James J. Cozine. *Saving the Big Thicket: From Exploration to Preservation, 1685-2003*. Denton, Tx: University of North Texas Press, 2004, 223-256. (No. 4 in the Temple Big Thicket Series.)

[33] Nathalie H. Wiest. *Canoing and Kayaking Houston Waterways*. College Station, Tx: Texas A&M University Press, 2012, 75-79.

[34] Nature preserves in the western Big Thicket include: the Demuth Sanctuary (617 acres, Liberty County, Houston Audubon Society); Winters Bayou Preserve (130.6 acres, San Jacinto County, Houston Audubon Society); Little Thicket Nature Sanctuary (655 acres, San Jacinto County, Houston Outdoor Nature Club); Lake Houston Wilderness Park (4986 acres, Harris-Montgomery Counties, City of Houston); Big Creek Scenic Area (1460 acres, San Jacinto County, maintained by Texas Forestry Association).

[35] Nature preserves in the eastern Big Thicket include: Patroon Bayou Mitigation Bank (presently 479 acres, Sabine County, Texas Conservation Fund); Caney Creek Nature

Park (24 acres, Newton County, City of Newton); Little Rocky Preserve (137 acres, Jasper County, Nature Conservancy); Siecke State Forest (1722 acres, Newton County, Texas Forestry Association).

[36] The areas currently protected along the Neches River beginning North of the Big Thicket National Preserve include: Angelina-Neches Wildlife Management Area (managed by U.S. Corps of Engineers); Angelina National Forest; Upland Island Wilderness Area (in Angelina National Forest); Alabama Creek Wildlife Management Area (in Davy Crockett National Forest); Neches River National Wildlife Refuge. For a more detailed account of these areas and the Neches river more broadly cf. Gina Donovan. *Neches River User Guide.* College Station, Tx: Texas A&M University Press, 2009, 83. For a brilliant textual and photographic survey of the Neches River, cf. F. E. Abernethy. *Let the River Run Wild!* Photos. Adrian F. Van Dellen. Nacogdoches, Tx: Stephen F. Austin State University Press, 2013, 152.

[37] The writing of this article has turned up several interesting questions which cannot be dealt with in these pages, but which deserve further investigation. Among these are: 1. The question of what the early Spanish soldiers, government officials and padres thought of the Big Thicket region. I am unable to find data on this issue. 2. The southern boundary of the Big Thicket is relatively clear. The northern boundary is less so. This later question involves the longleaf pine and the extent to which the longleaf-bluestem range, in its southern extent, was considered part of the original Big Thicket. 3. Lumber company records could be used to determine the actual size and species (e.g. pines or hardwoods) in the Big Thicket area. It must be possible, in this regard, to find numerous photos of large or "champion" trees.

INDEX

About the author

Pete A.Y. Gunter holds degrees in philosophy from Cambridge University and Yale University and has written widely in French and American philosophy.

Past president of the Big Thicket Association and chairman of the Big Thicket Coordinating Committee, he has written two books on the Big Thicket, *The Big Thicket*, 1971 and *The Big Thicket, an Ecological Reevaluation*, 1993.

Founding chairman of the Department of Philosophy at the University of North Texas, he was instrumental with Max Oelschlaeger in creating the first program in philosophy and ecology in the United States.

www.ingramcontent.com/pod-product-compliance
Lightning Source LLC
Chambersburg PA
CBHW052039280526
45791CB00010B/3016